Letters from Yellowstone

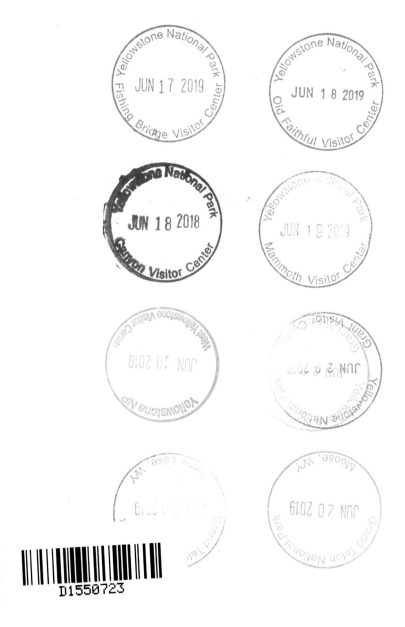

Letters from Yellowstone
30th Anniversary Edition

By Jim Carrier

The Denver Post's "Rocky Mountain Ranger"

Illustrations by Robert Spannring

- - - -

Foreword by George Robinson NPS

Afterword by Rocky Barker © 2018

Epilogue by Amy Carrier

First published as serial in the Denver Post ©1986

Book published by Roberts Rinehart Inc ©1987
Boulder, Colorado
ISBN 0-911797-37-8 (Cloth)
0-011797-38-6 (Paper)
Library of Congress catalog card number 87-61978

30th Anniversary Edition by Ranger Media ©2018
ISBN 9780911707381
41 Sky Drive, Burlington, VT 05408

To Amy, who will inherit the Earth

CONTENTS

ACKNOWLEDGEMENTS

These letters were written on a newspaper deadline, three times a week for a period of four months. Except for minor changes, they appear just as they did in the *Denver Post* in the summer and winter of 1986.

To the extent that they read well and contribute to an understanding of Yellowstone, credit must go to Gay Cook, Metropolitan Editor of the *Denver Post*, who edited the copy and listened to my cries from the wilderness, and to Managing Editor Tony Campbell who molded the "letters" concept and kept me in the mold.

I am indebted to the National Park Service staff at Yellowstone, especially Greg Kroll, John Varley, Anita Varley, Amy Vanderbilt, George Robinson and Bob Barbee. I hope it is obvious, to those people named in the stories, that I appreciated their help too.

My thanks to Robert Spannring for the use of his illustrations. www.robertspannring.com. And to Rick Rinehart, founder of Roberts Rinehart, Inc. Publishers, who saw in these letters the makings of a book and published it in 1987.

Finally, thanks to David Hall, editor of the *Denver Post*, who gave me the extraordinary job of *The Rocky Mountain Ranger*, and to Greg Moore and Dean Singleton who granted me rights to re-publish my work as the *Ranger.*

FOREWORD
to the
30th Anniversary Edition

Yellowstone is both a real place, an idea, and a state-of-mind. It can be a powerful elixir for us — the kind of place where author Barry Lopez has suggested that we can renegotiate our contracts with nature.

I had gone to Yellowstone with my father when I was a youngster, but I only remembered seeing some of its popular icons — geysers, Yellowstone Lake, Mammoth Hot Springs, some bears. Like many folks, my visit was cursory and superficial. I did not return to Yellowstone until the last few years of my career, and it was only then that I began to see that there was much more to this wonderland than the things that I had dreamed about and seen in my youth. Of course, there were hundreds of facts and figures to learn — many of which I soon forgot — but each day in Yellowstone brought new and precious fragments of thought and feeling that began to merge into a deeper understanding of meaning and place.

No human thought or actions have sculpted its features, or filled its ecological niches with abundant and diverse life forms. Here there is a rhythm to nature — a subtle flow of energy that Eastern philosophers call chi — that links all things. In Yellowstone, wild things move to a different cadence than we do. It is slow, measured, and harmonious. Here, natural process is like a Feng Shui master, arranging all of the elements in the house of nature in the most harmonious way. In these mountains, nature has woven a complex fabric of shapes, hard and soft, large and small; a network of lines crossing lines; angles folded upon angles; circles within circles; a full spectrum of colors; the basic pattern of natural order that Zen philosophers refer to as li.

Parks are public places, but the encounters people have in them are private and very personal. We react to our visits in special and different ways. Perhaps without realizing it we seek places and experiences that foster our reconnection with nature. We search for fundamental truths about natural process. Here, in the real world of geysers and grizzly bears, We find benchmarks against which we can measure the accelerated pace of our lives and times.

During my career in the National Park Service, which included 10 years in Yellowstone, I had ample time to develop my own sense of values, a feeling of my place in nature's scheme of things; to nurture an understanding of the importance of wild places; to learn a good deal about the machinery of nature and to see it working.

Some say that to "Do Yellowstone" we must see Old Faithful, Yellowstone Lake, The Grand Canyon. We must add a dipper, and a Clark's nutcracker to our life list, and we must learn the scientific names of Douglas fir and white bark pine. We must get close to a bison and a moose.

Still, writer and observer of nature John Fowles has said that these things act ". . .as an equivalent of the camera viewfinder. . .it destroys or curtails certain possibilities of seeing, apprehending and experiencing. . .Naming things is always implicitly categorizing and therefore collecting them, attempting to own them. . ." To name things is not necessarily to know them. one may never see all of the icons of the park, may never learn — and quickly forget — scientific names, yet if they take the time, take full advantage of the moment, they can apprehend its essential nature.

Too often, in our haste to stay with an itinerary — with our concentration on the past, or the future, rather than with mindfulness of the present, the possibilities of the moment — we see the form, but fail to experience the essence. Often we are driven by the imperative of the trail. It tells us that only designated routes lead to significant or especially scenic places, and that our experience will be incomplete if we fail to get to those destinations. In our myopic focus on the end of the trail, we fail to make hundreds of pleasant serendipitous discoveries along the way. A cursory visit limited to park roads, visitor centers, and developed areas, and a focus on the icons that conventional wisdom identifies with the park, conspire to make one's experience less meaningful.

Eastern philosophers say that the laws of nature and its processes — the machinery of the physical world — is Tao or The Way. They believe that in all things that exist there is form and essence. Form is outer: it can be seen, felt, weighed, measured. Essence is contained: it cannot be touched, counted, timed — and yet, it exists, and is that which sustains and animates form. Form without essence is lifeless. Essence cannot be manifested without form. In all things there are complementary opposites, yin and yang, life and death, male and female, light and darkness, winter and summer, flood and drought, matter and spirit. At the heart of science is the act of measurement. Something may be beautiful, emotionally moving, meaningful, and relevant, but if it cannot be put on a scale, or in a flask, if its length, width, and volume cannot be determined, it is of little interest to science. The essence of things can only be calculated in intangible personal terms.

We have an unspoken covenant with Yellowstone. To fully experience it, we must come to understand and appreciate it, to see Nature's pattern, to apprehend its meanings. When we allow the place to envelop us, we can feel its rhythm, the flow of its energy. We can see the beautiful complexity of Nature revealed. We can sense its palpable wild spirit. We can listen to its countless stories told in opposites of light and shadow, birth and death, winter and summer. We can have a perfect moment in a perfect place.

Seattle, a prominent Chief of the Duwamish and Suquamish tribes, once said "Take nothing but memories, leave nothing but footprints." It is an entreaty to park visitors uttered by hundreds of park rangers and interpreters. Experience, enjoy, and learn about this wonderland but leave it unimpaired.

Some places and things in Yellowstone shout for attention; others speak in whispers. But all of them reveal their essence only to those who take time to venture away from roads and developed areas, into the heart of the park. It is there that serendipitous discoveries are made, where one can come to truly understand the meaning of wilderness, the connections among living creatures, come upon the hidden and little-known places and hear the sounds of wild critters, the wind, a distant rockfall, the voice of a mountain stream. It is in these locations that a person can experience an epiphany, a sudden revelation of meaning.

Jim Carrier "did Yellowstone" the right way. He didn't snap a few pictures and rush to his next destination on a too short vacation. He took time. He left the trail. He heard Yellowstone's shouts and its whispers. He saw the form, but discovered the essence. His footprints are probably long gone, but his memories are recorded here with the skill of a seasoned and curious journalist. Enjoy them.

George Robinson, *Chief of Interpretation*
Yellowstone National Park (ret.)

JUNE

JUNE 1

\- - -

Packing for a summer in Yellowstone National Park didn't take much thought — good shoes, cotton and wool, Gore-Tex on the outside: the right combination to keep cool and warm and dry. It was simple — compared to the assignment. My job, for the next three months, was to find out what Yellowstone meant to us.

I was to live there, eat, sleep and breathe it. I was to talk with hundreds of people who use it, who live around it, who make their living from it. I would explore the park, the old inns, the geyser fields, the backcountry. On foot, boat, horseback, in my Jeep on the clogged summer roads.

And then, in a series of "letters," several a week in *The Denver Post*, I would try to capture it all in words. It was a dream assignment. An already wonderful job — roaming the Rockies, trying to explain the West — had hit pay dirt.

People I told about Yellowstone turned green. They envisioned a vacation, fishing and barbecues. Their next question was invariably: Is there enough material for a whole summer? Won't readers get tired of it?

Truthfully, the thought of trying to "capture" Yellowstone felt like trying to capture the falls on the Yellowstone River with a bucket. There weren't enough superlatives: the first, the biggest, the best known, a park that would just fit between Denver and Colorado Springs and cross the Continental Divide, too.

Yellowstone was the model for national parks world-wide. It was the crown jewel of America's national parks, and at times it appeared tarnished. That's why it swirled in controversy — because it was so important. It was a lightning rod for environmental issues and solutions nationwide. There wasn't an environmental group — or citizen, for that matter — without views about Yellowstone. And this summer, as America turned inward, they would be there. Three million was the projection. It was a great playground, safe from terrorists.

But in that vast wilderness, there was concern that man was making a mess. That this breeding ground for so many wild and rare species was being overrun and mismanaged. We had slaughtered the wolves with good intention. Now what were we doing to the grizzly? I had more questions than answers, and precious little knowledge. I knew it was home to Old Faithful and grizzlies. And I knew, from reading the news, that it was the vortex for man's attempt to manage wilderness — itself a contradiction in terms.

Fortunately, by devoting a summer to the park, I could better understand and explain those issues. But, I was warned by editors not to use the word ecosystem, which is what Yellowstone is. And I was worried, too, that all issues and no play would make "Letters" a dull tome. So I resolved to do both. What better place to learn fly fishing?

But no amount of thoughts of a summer fishing could relax my anxiety. That's my nature, until I hit the road. I could only go there and begin. So I packed my stuff and took off, to spend a summer writing letters from Yellowstone.

JUNE 3

- - -

It was snowing when I entered the park. Remnant squalls from a storm that had left its winter mark on the Absaroka Range and drenched early wheat on the Plains.

I drove in from the east, through Cody, Wyo., with the mountains in the distance, breaking off great clumps of clouds that blocked the setting sun before sailing overhead. Pockets of showers were still swirling in side canyons. Higher up, the peaks were lost in blizzards.

It is a Western landscape here, wide and high, with buttes shaped like giant molars set in green, forested gums. Rivers roiling toward me, banked by pale green cottonwoods. Snow still showing on the higher peaks, forming sandstone parfaits.

The valley of the Shoshone is a grand way to enter Yellowstone National Park. You drive first through a state park and a national forest, which buffer the park from commercial spoilage. What little private land there is, with log homes and meadows of horses, is insignificant in the vastness. The "Last Chance" gas sign is soon forgotten. Through Shoshone National Forest I drove, twisting with the river, rising beside it, just as the pioneers did on foot.

I had been in Yellowstone only once before — as a tourist in the summer. Thrilled by Old Faithful, disgusted with traffic, angry at cars that piled up at buffalo stops, but the first to stop when I was the first to see a moose.

This journey would take me through it for an entire summer. I'd join crowds at the geysers, I'd walk and camp in back-country wilderness. I'd talk with park managers, scientists, environmentalists, hitchhikers and drivers of Winnebagos. Everywhere I would ask, what does Yellowstone mean to us? I would write what I found in these letters. It would be, for me, a journal of discovery.

The road climbed abruptly past Buffalo Bill's original hunting lodge and snow hit the windshield thick and hard.

There was no one to greet me at the gate. Only signs: Tire chains or snow tires advisable. Travel at your own risk. Road closed West Thumb to Old Faithful. West Yellowstone 83 miles. Road may not be passable at night during storms. I turned on the heat.

The woods on either side were a dark, jumbled mess of wilderness management. Snow blew from escarpments cut in the drifts, and piled between hemlocks that hugged the narrow road.

Danger, the sign said, slide area. No stopping next two miles. I was between a snow cliff on my right, three times the height of the Cherokee, and a drop-off on the left. It was guarded by snapped wooden posts and broken cables.

The road turned down, toward Yellowstone Lake. I smelled sulphur. The sky brightened in the west. The lake was frozen except for the very edge where two ducks floated.

It was nearly dark now, and I was alone except for great hulks that loomed suddenly, buffalo or rocks, I couldn't tell. A nearly full moon came through the clouds. Just as abruptly the snow began. I started down a hill. The snow swirled, stopped and swirled again. I could not see the yellow line. In the headlights the snow came straight at me. It twisted. I jerked the wheel. I opened the window for sound, something to break the spell. It didn't help. I turned the lights off. The swirling stopped.

At Madison Junction I turned right and the moon shone again, behind me. Through the West Yellowstone gate I drove, into town, its neon quiet.

Small lights were on in the cabin, and door left open. At midnight, in chilled air, I unpacked, still dizzy with vertigo. I built a small fire, opened a beer and crawled into bed. I made it through one short Steinbeck story before falling asleep.

JUNE 6

From where I sleep, I can reach the log walls of this cabin, and I lay here the first morning in Yellowstone, touching the wood and studying the room.

The logs are lodgepole pine, rough hewn, 8 inches in diameter, and spaced apart 2 inches, the style when this cabin was built in the early 1920s. The gap between them is filled with mortar and painted white so that each log stands out. On the inside, they are varnished to a sheen, and on the outside painted a dark brown.

There is just enough room in here to stand beside the double bed, with room at the foot for a straight-backed chair, a chest of drawers and a mirror. The "closet" is a rod stuck cater-cornered between the log walls.

Near the foot of the bed is a window, wide and low, covered by a burlap curtain and valance. The view through it is unimportant — another building an arm's reach away, and scrap lumber piled in the alley — so it is boarded over. Its real value lies inward, as a balance to the room and connection to the outside.

The cabin is well proportioned and man-size. It is a basic rectangle, with the bedroom and kitchen splitting one end, beyond which is a screened-in porch. I have stacked my camping gear there. The other end is the living room, basically square, the logs exposed and open to the roof's peak.

There is a wood-burning stove, a TV with cable, two old rocking chairs, old lamps and a fold-out sofa. For night lights, there are two miniature covered wagons, pulled by plastic horses, the wagons lit by electric bulbs.

The cabin has about it a lived-in feel, warm and worn. The steel bed squeaks, the steel roof speaks, in rain. It has been home to its owners since it was built. Tom and Dorit Herman, operators of the Wagon Wheel Trailer Park behind me, plan to winter here now that he is retired, and then each summer move into their travel trailer, so they can rent the cabin to romantics like me.

I spent the first day unpacking, arranging, lining shelves with early provisions. The storm had cleared and the sky was bright blue. It was warm in the sun at this altitude, but in the shadow of the cabin in the morning, ice still floated on top of the rain barrel.

At the Roundup Market, I bought staples: beans, flour, bacon, bananas, decaffeinated coffee, potato chips and Oreo cookies. I had brought everything else important with me: flannel shirts and jeans, books and my banjo.

I set up my writing computer on a small table in the living room, facing the logs. Next to it is a big old Philco radio standing in the corner. It still works, but picks up only one station, the daytime West Yellowstone signal, a mix of country and rock. Above the desk sits a cow skull and a Charlie Russell print, one of three on the walls.

I set up my record player with a few of the records I brought, bluegrass and Beethoven, and staked a shelf of books: *Walden, Lake*

Woebegon Days, books by Truman Capote, Carlos Castaneda and Richard Bach. And I began what I expect to be a huge library of books on Yellowstone: *Bear Attacks*, *Track of the Grizzly*, and *Playing God.*

Then, nearly ready for work, I stapled a relief map of Yellowstone National Park to the bathroom door, below another skull. I taped a larger geological survey map to Masonite and propped it in a corner. I expect, by summer's end, to have covered the map, first in this cabin, then out in the park, which lies a half mile from the door.

From this base, the view, like the one through the bedroom window, will provide a sense both of what is out there, and in here, in me.

JUNE 8

- - -

The first green-uniform ranger you see at Yellowstone National Park is a ticket taker with a cash box — and patience, humor and "knowledge of things human and divine," as wisdom was once defined.

"Is this the way to California?"

"When do the elk turn into deer?"

"What kind of uniforms do the cattle guards wear?"

Those are the questions they remember, these seasonal men and women, whose work is so deadly predictable: "Hello. There's a $2 entry fee. It's good for seven days, and it's good for Grand Teton National Park, too. Thank you."

Hundreds of times a day, they repeat the smile, the hello, the litany. And answers to the usual questions: "Where's the bears?" Where's the bathrooms? How far to Old Faithful? When does Old Faithful go off?"

They stand there, guardians of this great treasure, and bear the brunt, sometimes, of a taxpayer's ire because he thinks $2 per vehicle is too much or because he has to pay $1 to run his snow machine in the park.

Stewart Orgill remembers when the fee was $3, back in the '50s when he started with the Park Service as summer help. Now he's in charge of the West Gate, right outside West Yellowstone, a ruddy Scot with particular pride in the detail it takes to run an entrance station year-round.

In his office he showed me a manual with a history of fees at Yellowstone. Admission was first charged in 1915, the year they allowed the first autos. The fee for "runabouts for single-seated cars" was $5. A five-passenger horseless carriage was $7. A seven-passenger monster was charged $10. In 1918, a uniform fee of $7.50 was charged; this was lowered to $3 in 1926 and to $2 in 1970.

West is the busiest of the five gates at Yellowstone. Last year it handled one third of the 2.2 million people, one-third of the 772,000 vehicles, three-fourths of the 36,000 snow machines, and nearly half of the $617,834 the park collected in entry fees.

The money goes to the federal Land and Water Conservation Fund, not the park, whose budget is $12.1 million. The Park Service has a bill before Congress to charge $10 at Yellowstone and return half the money to parks.

I read somewhere that 30 percent of U.S. citizens have seen Yellowstone. Sitting beside an entrance booths, I could believe it. I saw America pass before me: a station wagon with five kids, seniors in a sedan from Idaho, an Ohio van, a Montana Suburban, a Brat 4x4 with fresh Alaskan mud, a religious group in 12 cars, and RVs of every size imaginable A Winnebago Chieftain from North Carolina had to pull in its mirrors to get through.

On July 4, they back up clear to town and honk, their vacation schedule ticking away. Shaving five seconds off each ticket sale can make a big difference in tempers, said Orgill, who operates four booths during peak periods. In the winter, one booth can handle the hundreds of snow machines that skid in each morning on unplowed roads. They've had as many as 2,000 machines in one day. The average is 800.

The day I watched, 1,790 vehicles pulled through the West gate. The record is last July 5 — 2,975.

Most of the encounters were routine. Two dollars, change, and the usual exchange. There were a few that rangers remembered a year later.

"Where's the place with the big heads?"

"Where's the redwood tree you can drive through?"

Politely, with a smile, they were told, wrong park, wrong state.

JUNE 12

- - -

I first saw them wading barefoot in Obsidian Creek, a family of four, the father holding the little girl's hand, the boy brave and on his own, not wanting Mom's help. It was a hot day and the water felt good.

By the time I got turned around and stopped, they had crossed the road and were kneeling together before an elk, deep in discussion about comparative biology.

"Cows have black spots," said David Monson, who is 4.

"It sure smells different than Iowa," said his father, Terry.

"It doesn't smell like pigs," added Lisa, his mother.

This was the first trip to Yellowstone for Mom and the kids. Terry, a dentist in Fenton, Iowa, had been before. It was his favorite park. "Our friends were amazed I wanted to come back."

They had been to the Black Hills, seen Mount Rushmore, stopped by the Custer Battlefield, taken a raft trip on the Shoshone and then driven their Chevy Celebrity into Yellowstone. They will hit the Tetons and the Cheyenne rodeo before this trip is over. In the fall, they may come back.

"I like seeing the wild animals and knowing that they're safe," said Lisa. "I really want to see a bear."

Terry had been here 20 years before, when the black bears begged at the roadside and the campers were bumper-to-bumper, waiting their turn to feed them. He liked animals in the wild and primitive parks. But with the family, Yellowstone was a nice compromise. There were animals and geysers and motels.

"You know when you go in a place like this, it is pretty much the way it was 100 years ago," he said. "It's nice to look at it and know that Lewis and Clark saw the same thing. And it will be the same 100 years from now. Not that it's breathtaking, but it's always here."

I left them with the elk and gave Ray Cox a ride. He was hitchhiking from Texas to Alaska and didn't know anything about Yellowstone. In fact, he would have thumbed his way up the interstate and missed the Tetons, Yellowstone and Glacier National Park if it hadn't been for people pointing the way.

"I thought Yellowstone was a big, overgrown roadside park," he said.

He was a Bible scholar. The Word had lifted him from his drunkenness, and he had memorized 7,000 verses since. He had packed five Bibles and several other scriptural texts, but mailed them home because they were too heavy. Now he walked with a King James, reading to himself, memorizing.

In his huge pack he carried the usual stuff for cross-country hiking: a stove, a sun shower, a gallon of water, toilet paper, a sleeping bag. He also had a camera and tripod, a spear made of copper tubing from his plumbing shop, a box of felt-tip markers for the Bible, and an index card file with Bible verses organized by subject. He could look up "affliction" or "judgment" or "strength." On the outside of his pack he had drawn a fish.

I told him about the Church Universal and Triumphant that owned the former Forbes ranch north of the park and about a restaurant it ran near Gardiner. I also asked him for a verse to describe the park. He thought a minute.

"There's a Psalm. The heavens declare the glory of God and the skies show his handiwork. King James says firmament, but nobody knows what that means so I just say sky."

We drove by the Mammoth Hot Springs. He didn't want to see it. I took him to the north gate, and lifted his pack from the trunk.

"I can really see God's hands here," he said. "Where did you say that church was?"

JUNE 15

- - -

Most of the famous attractions of Yellowstone National Park are adjacent to the road, a 350-mile two-lane blacktop with lots of potholes and patches and turnouts for parking.

The road is laid out in a huge figure 8, pretty much in the center of the park. The lower loops runs by Yellowstone Lake and Old Faithful. The upper loop skirts the Grand Canyon and Mammoth Hot springs. Between these points lie broad valleys of wildlife, rivers and waterfalls, wet meadows, even petrified trees.

Because the road to these spots is cut through seemingly endless forests of lodgepole pines, it's easy to view the whole park as petrified, a curiosity preserved in some pristine state, framed by a windshield.

The animals seem tame, so used to cars are they, and they become part of the landscape, to be photographed or ignored. The park becomes a giant drive-through zoo.

When I first arrived I saw it that way. I would drive by the animals, for buffalo and elk no longer excited me. I would swing around tourists who stopped for them and would rush on to important appointments. One of the first was with a naturalist.

Jack de Golia was a short, dark man with a beard and features somewhere between Lincoln and Castro. A former actor, his face was rubber, and he was not bashful about screwing it into grimaces to make a point or get a laugh.

We took a short walk, and he showed me signs of spring, the purple larkspur, the yellow arrowhead balsam root that blankets the park. He talked of the smell of death, when carcasses of elk and buffalo, winter-killed, begin to rot. He showed me the bones of an elk that he had used on his walks here, to explain the cycle of life. They were dry and bleached now, a year old.

"The big change in spring is that there are more human beings around," he said. "The roadways lose their wilderness feeling."

I stopped and looked at him. "Do you really get a sense of wilderness from your car, on the road?"

"Yes," he said. I couldn't agree.

More than a week later, toward evening on a Sunday, I took another drive through the park. I did not hurry. I kept the radio off. I drove and watched and thought. For long stretches I saw no one.

I drove up the Gibbon River, across the Central Plateau, the middle of the figure 8, and north across Dunraven Pass into the upper loop.

I just missed seeing a moose and her calf in one clearing. The traffic jam was dispersing.

A few minutes later, traffic halted again. A black bear and her big cub were less than 100 yards away, on a hillside, browsing. I stepped out and took a picture. A fellow beside me said, "The last time I saw a black bear it was along the roadside begging. This is far better." Bears are rarely seen today.

Farther along, I stopped for a group of photographers standing by the road. They had been waiting 10 hours for a grizzly bear and her two cubs to reappear along Antelope Creek.

Early that morning the grizzly had chased an elk calf into the woods; the cry of death could be heard from the road. The elk cow had then chased the bear cubs across the road, and mama had followed to retrieve them. They returned and bedded down for the day in a grove by the creek, probably with the meat.

As we watched, many cars zipped by. Some drivers slowed and inquired, but seeing nothing, drove on. I waited two hours, until dusk, and the cubs never showed. But while we were watching a pair of grizzlies appeared on a high ridge, a dark male and lighter female.

Through spotting scopes we could see them court, touch muzzles, begin an unsuccessful mount, and sit leaning against each other. I thought of what Jack de Golia had said. Here, standing on a gravel shoulder, I was witnessing a natural act in the wild.

Later I learned that at Old Faithful the same day, an elk had given birth by a sidewalk, 1,000 yards from the inn. A man had videotaped the event while children watched. Someone showed me the spot and the elk, now grazing and nursing near the Firehole. I could have seen it, given patience and timing, the keys to catching the unpredictable. I could have closed the circle of death and life in one day. I began to appreciate one of Yellowstone's charms.

You can drive through, never leave your car, and see nature in a windshield postcard. The roads are good for that, and many people want nothing more.

Or, you can stop, step outside, and sometimes see the wilderness by the road.

JUNE 17

Yellowstone is often called a park besieged, but I never really understood what that meant until I went to a meeting of the Greater Yellowstone Coalition.

It would take a lifetime of living here to be exposed to the range of opinions I heard. At one session, scientists presented papers on viable populations, cumulative-effects models, ecosystem management and grizzly bear habitat.

Out in the lobby, at table after table, members of the environmental coalition stacked literature, on ferrets and wolves, eagles and bears, each, it seemed, more endangered than the last. There were lobbyists from the Madison Gallatin Alliance, the National Audubon Society, the Bear Creek Council and Defenders of Wildlife, each more earnest than the one before.

It reminded me of my first trip to Yellowstone years ago. In a marsh north of the lake, a moose was grazing. Tourists with cameras, ignoring common sense, had formed a circle around him. If he raised his head, cameras would go off. And if he took a step forward, the crowd moved with him.

Yellowstone National Park today is in a similar circle, surrounded geographically and figuratively by people and institutions of varying interests and demands. While it is 2 million acres big, it is an ecological island, stuck like a postage stamp on the upper lefthand corner of Wyoming, surrounded by four national forests, another park and three states.

Yellowstone's mission is different. The park preserves its land; the national forests are open to many uses — recreation, timbering, oil and gas drilling. As big as Yellowstone is, there is now a feeling that it should have been 6 million acres, big enough for free-roaming bears, big enough for migrating bison, big enough to protect the geysers from thermal drilling threatened outside its borders.

Unfortunately, that area is now in the hands of 25 political jurisdictions and private landowners. And their interests are not always environmental.

A park proposal to reintroduce the wolf is opposed by Montana cattlemen. A plan to close a campground in bear habitat is opposed by businessmen in Wyoming. Pushing park officials from the other side are dozens of environmental groups, each with a pet agenda.

And then there are scientists, who themselves can't agree on what needs doing. Between May and September, 100 short days, the park is overrun by researchers, studying bats, boiling water and butterflies. The grizzly is especially studied. Some would argue it is studied to death. Their findings fuel more debate on what is right for Yellowstone.

"There is no decision we can make that does not create controversy," said Greg Kroll, the park's harried spokesman.

Ultimately, "biopolitics still dominates what we do," said a park official. It was a word new to me, but appropriate.

In many ways, the Greater Yellowstone Coalition is the park's best friend. It brings to one place the viewpoints of the circle. And it pushes the concept that the park cannot survive as an island.

The idea has now reached Washington. Last fall, Congress held hearings on public policy around the park. Computer studies to save the grizzly now are being done in the forests surrounding Yellowstone. By adding up the effects of such things as logging and skiing — up to now considered independently — officials hope they can better assess the possible damage to bear life.

Thanks to the coalition, largely, the different jurisdictions and constituencies around the park are beginning to talk and listen, and understand that their best interests lie in common.

But for Yellowstone to survive, these people in the circle have to join hands.

JUNE 22

- - -

I found my old sea legs the other day, a long way from the sea, on a body of water as temperamental as the north Atlantic and just as deadly.

I was standing in the stern of a 25-foot Bertram, my legs braced between the transom and the engine cover. I could feel the throb of the twin Mercruisers with one knee and the pitch of Yellowstone Lake with the other.

Fifty feet away and closing, a green 20-foot cruiser crammed with a family was bobbing helplessly. Their motor had seized. The owner balanced on the bow with a line.

I forgot that I was on a wilderness lake in the middle of Yellowstone National Park. It was more like duty with the Coast Guard off Nantucket.

My skipper was boat ranger Rick Fey, one of two park rangers who patrol the lake. When I met him at Bridge Bay, near the campground, I was surprised to find a full-blown marina, with 35-foot cruisers and sailboats moored in 120 slips. It had been dug out of an old marsh.

The ranger station was more nautical than rustic, the usual fare in the park. And there were sea gulls and the smell of fish and outboard exhaust — here on a high lake in Wyoming.

Boats have been here since the turn of the century. A steamship once carried dusty stagecoach riders from West Thumb to the Lake Hotel. Fey estimates there are maybe 80 to 100 motorboats a day on a lake that's 110 miles around. Tourists rent 16-foot boats with 25-horse motors to fish or take the kids for a ride. Last year, 2,794 brought their own boats, half of them motorized. Many of them camp at back-country sites near the southern portion of the lake.

You can't water-ski on Yellowstone Lake, and it's too cold to swim. It was 34 degrees at two feet the day I spent with Fey.

As we cruised out in thick fog on the opening day of fishing season, Fey said his job is to protect visitors from the lake as well as to protect the lake from them. He checked for fishing licenses and made sure people weren't over their limit — two cutthroat trout, under 13 inches.

He showed me the spot, directly across the lake from Bridge Bay, where a boat swamped in high winds and tossed two boys and a father into the water last summer. The father drowned. The boys were dead of hypothermia by the time they were on shore, 100 yards away.

"I'll never forget those little kids," Fey said. "When I put them in the bag, I said, "Darn, is there anything I could have done?""

Fey, tall, a little sunburned, with curly brown hair and probably the only ranger in the park with sunglasses hung around his neck, is a schoolteacher from Illinois. In 1973 he and his wife, also a teacher, came to Yellowstone on vacation. They spotted a fire tower and asked about a job. They've been coming back summers ever since. They're both rangers. Margie in a car patrol and Rick on the lake, and they now call Aspen their winter home.

It was late afternoon near Storm Point when we spotted the waving red flag and mirror flash and approached the green cruiser. When the man threw the line I caught it, snapped it to a bridle, and played out the towline as Fey edged forward.

The boat's occupants waved their arms in joy. It would be two hours to port, nearly sunset, but they were safe. I climbed back to sit with Fey on the flying bridge.

"If I had worked my eight hours, these people would have been on the rocks," he said. "The lake is going to throw out stuff that the best boatman in the best boat can't handle. Waves of six to eight feet are not unusual."

He told of rescues he has made at midnight, using the radar to steer past islands, and how, each night, he "tucks in the lake" with a big swing around, checking for boats in trouble and the back-country campsites.

Having dropped the green cruiser at the marina and filled out the necessary paperwork, Fey boarded again. It was dusk. He throttled the big inboard to 4,100 rpm and took off. We shivered in our float coats.

I watched the sky paint the water, blue with yellow and a pink overlay. We flushed a pelican that beat its great delta wings, outdistancing us. As we passed Stevenson Island, the water turned smooth. In a last hurrah, the angel hair showed coral against the cobalt sky, above the black serrated horizon of forest. All was quiet.

JUNE 24

- - -

I went looking for bear the other day — grizzly bear.

My guide was Steve French, a man who will see more bears in Yellowstone than anybody this summer, because he goes where they are. He agreed to let me come along.

We hit Hayden Valley, smack in the middle of the park, about 6 a.m. and were just up off the pavement when he showed me the first tracks. Dried in mud, one paw measured about 4 3/4 inches across. Another was slightly smaller.

As we walked west, we climbed sage-covered knolls, up and down. At the top of each, Steve would put his finger to his lips, take off his cowboy hat, and creep to the crest.

The valley was waking up. We heard coyotes, and the flutter of ducks on the Yellowstone River. Each hill we climbed was lit at the top by the sun rising behind us. We stopped to rest often.

I was carrying a huge wood tripod, and Steve was carrying a 16mm movie camera, with a lens about as long as his leg. We both shouldered backpacks, and carried binoculars. As we caught our breath. he talked about his favorite subject.

"I've seen 75 grizzlies this year, in three weeks of looking. I know 42 different bears," he said. "The bears in Yellowstone are very healthy. We have a healthy breed that can be saved. We have a new bear that is not as fat. It's free and wild. It's behaviorally different than the garbage bears."

I had seen pictures in the 1960s of bears along the road, being fed everything imaginable by tourists. They poked their heads into cars, begged on their haunches. The scenes were known as "bear jams" and were as much a part of Yellowstone as Old Faithful.

I also had seen pictures of bears in the dumps of Yellowstone, waiting for the garbage trucks to show up. Up until 1941, the park had bleachers by dumps for nightly bear shows.

But the dumps were closed and the feeding stopped around 1970. A new philosophy swept wildlife managers. Not only was it aesthetically displeasing to see bears eating trash, it was dangerous.

Because they ate human food, carrying human scent, and sometimes held by a human hand, the bears became used to humans. And they lost their fear of man. Aggressive bears would tear through campgrounds, coolers and tents looking for more food. Inevitably, there were conflicts with people. Black bears, the bears along the road, would occasionally nibble a finger. Grizzles did far worse damage.

Steve French was a surgical resident at the University of Utah hospital in the late 1970s when he told me he watched as plastic surgeons took a flap of skin from the shoulder of Barrie Gilbert, a Utah biologist mauled at Yellowstone, to cover the missing left side of his face. After that, French got interested in studying bears. When the university contracted to run Yellowstone's clinic at Yellowstone Lake, French was sent for a two-week period. Thus began his love affair with Yellowstone and grizzlies.

"I learned about the grizzly bear, and I had the best teacher — the bear," he told me. "I read all the books and attended all the seminars. But the only way to observe and experience wildlife is to sit down and wait."

He showed me spring beauties popping their white flowers up after snow banks receded, yellow bells and biscuit root — all bear food. And he grinned when he found evidence that a bear had dug into a cache of yampa, buried by a pocket gopher.

Every few minutes, we scanned the sage for bear. He pointed to the spot of the infamous Trout Creek dump, the last dump to close in Yellowstone. "Now bears are congregating at trout streams," he said. "Today's generation is rediscovering the old food sources. They're chasing elk everywhere." Just a few days earlier, he had filmed a bear killing an elk calf.

I asked him why people didn't see bears along the road anymore. French said he had heard stories. But he didn't care to mire in the politics of the bear.

33

C'mon," he said, picking up his pack. "Let's go see some bears."

JUNE 26

- - -

Steve French looked like no doctor I'd ever seen.

Mountain man, maybe, with a long scruffy beard, a beat-up Stetson and an aw-shucks way of talking, a truck driver's boy from Texas. But not a respected emergency room chief from Evanston, Wyo., one-time medical chief of staff, marathon runner and all-around pillar of the community. What better company, I thought, in bear country?

We had spent a futile morning in Hayden Valley looking for grizzlies, but it was getting hot and unlikely they would appear from their daybeds in the trees. We would return again at sunset. On the way back to the pickup, French lectured me about bear attacks.

"A bear can kill a human at will," he said. "But they usually don't." Bears attack when they're threatened: a mother protecting her cubs, a bear defending a carcass, a bear surprised. Rarely is a bear just trying to eat you.

In Yellowstone's history, there have been hundreds of injuries and four deaths from bears. Last year there were no injuries. But in 1984, a woman was eaten by a grizzly that never was found. It was the kind of talk around a campfire that would send me to my bedroll with the willies — if I went at all.

That evening, a front was coming through. By the time we returned to the valley, rain was falling in sheets. I hunched beneath a parka and Steve crawled on the lee side of sagebrush.

"I hate to take out the poncho," said. "It's still packed up in the way I bought it. I hate to mess it up." He said it in that good-ole-boy Texas drawl.

A few nights before, he had been caught out here after dark and stumbled onto a grizzly with cubs. The sow charged to within 50 feet, stood up, turned and left.

I told him the bear would have spit him out as too hairy. He told me I could take comfort in knowing a bear would return me to the nitrogen cycle.

"It's important for the grizzly bear to have the capacity to kill and eat us," he said. "That may seem paradoxical for a doctor. But the fact that they do keeps us humble. We should see ourselves not as top of the heap, but as a cohabitant.

"We hold the grizzly bear in awe, not because of mythology, not because it stands and walks, not for its speed or dexterity. The reason is that it can kill and eat us. If it didn't it would be a 500-pound marmot."

Attempts to teach bears to fear man, he said, so-called aversive training being tried in Wyoming and Montana, were regrettable.

"They might as well take the gravity out of the mountains, the swiftness out of the streams, the heat out of the thermal areas. Let's pave it over so you won't turn an ankle. Let's sanitize Yellowstone."

Just then, the rain stopped and a rainbow appeared. The sky was so big that it was raining behind us and sunny ahead. Scattered throughout the valley, as far as we could see, were elk and buffalo, grazing.

"You see," Steve grinned. "Mother nature rewards those who suffer through harsher times."

Moments later we caught a glimpse of two bears in the distance. Just a tease in the glare of the setting sun. Then they were gone. We watched instead an elk herd below us. "Here comes kindergarten," Steve said. From out of nowhere came four calves, romping in play. They moved through the herd and found their mothers.

I got home at midnight, 20 hours after I started the day. Steve apologized for not doing better, but I reminded him of something he had said earlier.

"My end point is not to count grizzlies. My love is to go and enjoy grizzly country. And it's darn good country — about the best thing we have left."

For that one day, I was a cohabitant.

JUNE 29

- - -

My search for bears in Yellowstone was more than a curious safari.

I wanted to see them because they are so rare, because they are the essence of wildness. But also because I was nagged by the question: where are the bears? A question everyone asks when they drive through the gate and see the sign: "This is bear country." The answer was as elusive as the grizzles Steve French and I tried to find in Hayden Valley.

No one really knows how many bears are in Yellowstone. The park's estimate is about 200 grizzlies, but they never have been counted. The black bear population is anybody's guess. It may be as low as the grizzlies', but the black is not considered threatened.

The first real study of the Yellowstone grizzly began in 1959 when biologists realized the bear was in trouble. It was hunted outside the park. It had been forced to live on a smaller range. When it tangled with man or man's livestock it usually lost. Even within the park, "problem bears," those who had injured someone or were considered dangerous, were routinely killed. It always had been that way.

In 1937, a year in which there were 115 personal injuries and 81 cases of property damage, 41 black bears and 10 grizzlies were killed.

When the park closed the garbage dumps and stopped roadside feeding in 1968 the bears went wild. They rummaged through campgrounds, strolled into bordering towns, even walked onto the front porch of Old Faithful Inn. It begin a period they called "Bear Wars." Again, the bears lost.

Many were transplanted, trapped and drugged, carried away by trucks and helicopter. Most came back. They got two or three chances. After that they were killed. No one knows how many black bears were killed, but it is likely in the hundreds. Local people say the roads in the park went from being "lousy with bears" to bearless in one season.

As for the less visible grizzly, more than 100 were killed in the name of "control" between 1968 and 1984. Another 200 died in and around Yellowstone, mostly from hunting and poaching.

The last two of the garbage dump grizzlies were killed in Montana last year, 15 years after the park decided to create a wild and free-ranging bear. It was a dark period in wildlife management.

In Yellowstone now, every bear counts. Grizzlies have become a gauge of the biological health of the park.

They have also become a measure of the park's success in carrying out its mandate to preserve the park while providing for the pleasure of man. As a result, the bear exerts an influence far beyond its number.

Five to seven percent of Yellowstone's budget is devoted to the grizzly. A special office keeps track of bear sightings. Trails are closed to prevent bears from being chased away by hikers. Extraordinary efforts are taken to keep the park clean. Garbage is picked up twice a day. Rangers and a forest of signs warn visitors to keep their food away from bears. All-night patrols watch for coolers left out in campgrounds.

"Once rewarded with food, then it is only a matter of time before the bear is destroyed," said John Varley, the park's chief biologist. "Human-bear conflicts translate directly into dead bears."

JULY

JULY 1

- - -

They came from the East, driving their Detroit horses to Bill Cody's ranch to ride the real McCoy.

The write-up in the American Automobile Association guidebook brought them. It sounded romantic, this place on the North Fork. Cookouts and trail rides, just a skip and holler from Yellowstone.

It didn't seem to matter that it wasn't much more than a motel with a dining room, cabins by a creek, with a bunch of horses and kids called wranglers to lead them on trails along a creek called Nameit.

This was the Wild West.

"Is this sagebrush?" Richard Barth asked as we rode the low trail after supper. "Yup," I told him. Barth was a mystery writer, and sage didn't grow this high in Manhattan. He'd come for the sheer adventure of driving his family across America in an RV, a prospect that made their city friends gasp. They might as well have said they were headin' out with Lewis and Clark in an ox cart, in search of the Pacific.

They'd come, also, because of Bill Cody's granddad, the man they called Buffalo Bill. He took the West to the East when it was still a frontier. Winters he played himself in the first "westerns" in New York; summers he scouted the Indian territory for the cavalry. He built a town with his name, brought in Mormons to irrigate it, dug the first oil well and built a road to a new park 50 miles west called Yellowstone. And then he drove guests there, through the ruts, in a Stanley Steamer.

Bill Garlow remembers sitting on his granddad's lap, and being taken to his deathbed. A lot of years passed before he changed his name to Cody and decided to ride Buffalo Bill's coattails. He grew a white moustache and goatee, wore a fringe jacket, and pushed BB guns and motorhomes — "Bill Cody's home on the range." Then he settled down to run a little resort on the Cody road to Yellowstone and, just like his granddaddy, sell a little west to the easterners who passed by.

"The name of the game here is sales. Ninety-five percent of the time I'm selling. Giving them BS. Selling them an extra night, selling them a trail ride." In 11 years, he and his wife built their gross from $5,000 to $250,000.

"But that wasn't because I was the grandson of Buffalo Bill. It was because Barbara and I worked our tails off. My grandfather's name may have paid the electric bill. Buffalo Bill gave me enough bull to marry a gal 28 years younger who works 16 hours a day."

When the big RV from New York drove up, 73-year-old Bill Cody walked out in his blue denim sneakers to greet them by name. "Hi," he said to the kids. "I'm Uncle Bill." Then he hopped on his Yamaha four-wheeler to lead them to their cabin. For $200 a night, the Barths got a cabin, meals and trail rides.

After supper, family style, they went riding. Ilene Barth, a newspaper editor, rode, her new Banana Republic canvas-and-leather boots stuck in the stirrups. She'd bought them in Manhattan. Out in front, led by the wrangler from Kansas, was Morgan, the Barth's 6-year-old. He began the ride with the shout, "Daddy, your horse just pooped!"

"My son wasn't raised on the same thing I was — Tom Mix and Hopalong Cassidy," said Barth. "And so cowboys don't hold the same charisma. They're all brought up on robots now."

But you could see the West eat into Morgan's soul as the ride neared its end. The motor sound he made became a whistle. He asked for a cowboy hat and real boots. Tomorrow, he said, he wanted to hold the reins himself. And then he turned in his saddle, pointed a finger at his dad and said, "Stick 'em up."

JULY 3

- - -

"Look at those flowers. Smell!" Ron Blanchard yelled above the white water.

"See the wild roses. Take a deep breath."

We took our eyes off the waves and inhaled on command.

"Watch out for moose," he yelled. "OK, now paddle."

I tried to hold my feet out of the water. They were numb. The four boys from New England, my raft companions, were stoic.

"We'll bail when we stop," Ron said. "See the basalt, from the Yellowstone eruption. Look at the colors in there."

We looked this way and that, inhaled and felt, opened our senses to the wildness around us.

Since coming to Cody as a rodeo cowboy in the '70s, Ron Blanchard has soaked up the area, the history, the geography, the wildlife, the flowers. As he wrestled his big rubber raft down the North Fork of the Shoshone, he spit it all back, a naturalist with a paddle. He realized he couldn't rodeo forever. Two years on the Alaska pipeline gave him and his brother, 37 and 31 years old, the bankroll to begin a raft business.

"I'm in the outdoor recreation industry," he said. "There are lots of people working in Detroit factories or in front of Boston computer terminals 50 weeks a year. When they get away they don't have the physical ability to run a river. They need a professional to bring them out, to establish that link with nature."

The boys in front began to squeal, almost involuntarily, with each cold splash. The water had left Yellowstone during the night as snowmelt and was still icy.

We beached on a sandbar, and the lesson continued.

"Look, here's petrified wood. It's all over the place. See the moose tracks. They're fresh."

I could see the boys from the Bay opening up, slowing down. The submarine maker, particularly. He was whiter than the rest, older, his legs spotted with veins. Twice he thought he spotted an animal in the brush.

"This is like Narangansett Bay," he yelled as we shoved off into a new set of rapids. "Except this smells better."

"Teddy Roosevelt thought the area between Cody and Yellowstone was the most scenic 52 miles in the West," Ron said. "It's Yellowstone country all the way. But at 55 mph you don't appreciate it. Not until you float through it at 6 miles an hour. Yellowstone is a state of mind. There's a freedom and openness to it. How long you boys going to stay?"

"We were going to drive through it today," said one. They looked at each other.

"You really ought to stay, and take in a campfire or a slideshow by the naturalists," Ron said. "See how the basalt swept over harder rocks. Yellowstone built this country, geologically. The link is still there, but it's a commercial one."

The Blanchards and other river runners last year proposed raft trips inside Yellowstone. The park studied it and rejected it.

"There's always going to be controversy between gateway communities and environmentalists," said Ron. "As long as we have both, there will be a balance. There's always going to be that battle line between wilderness and more development."

He pointed to a campsite beside the river where his company, Wyoming River Trips, stops on their overnight trip. The Shoshone National Forest allows them two trips a day on the North Fork. Their most common trip is a two-hour float near downtown Cody. Last year they carried 6,000 people.

"It's the neatest thing to take a family down the river and expose them to a different lifestyle," Ron said. "They learn about themselves. You need time to explore inside."

By now the boys from Boston were rethinking their trip. We stopped for a long time to watch a bighorn sheep and her baby totter along a ridge above the river. Then it was time for lunch ashore, laid

43

out on a table cloth with wildflowers. After four hours on the river we were starved. We warmed in the sun, ate meat and cheese and fruit, and rerode the river in our talk.

"Boy, I'd like to die right here," said the sub builder.

When I last saw him he was standing beside the North Fork, pulling needles off an evergreen sprig and holding them to his nose.

JULY 6

- - -

I couldn't come to Yellowstone without sampling the Grand Tetons, the spectacular range and park to the south. But what to do there?

Like most tourists, I had driven through Jackson Hole a number of times, my eyes riveted to those peaks, rising abruptly from the Snake River and Jenny Lake. It's as classic a vista as you'll find in the Rockies, and I never tire of just looking.

I suppose I'd always thought of climbing them — the little boy in me wanting to top the rock. I was drawn to them. They beckoned. Yet I knew they were killers. Was that the lure? The Siren of the West?

Nice as the walks were around Jenny Lake, and the boat ride, and the grand vistas, it seemed there was no other way to experience the Tetons than to climb them. So I walked across a wooden footbridge spanning Cottonwood Creek and into a dark old building, its sign — "Exum Guide Service" — nearly hidden by bushes, and reserved a place in rock-climbing school.

I have to admit, though, that the idea that sounded so exciting then seemed stupid the day I drove down from Yellowstone. This wasn't going to be a Sunday hike. I was fussy, worrying about my clothes, the right shoes, my pack and gloves. I knew blizzards could strike. And winds could blow you off. The instructions mailed to me insisted on wool pants, wool or polypropylene underwear, wool gloves and rappelling gloves. I mean, this was serious.

I stopped to visit with Glenn Exum, the grand old man of climbing in the Tetons. He first climbed the Grand, the tallest peak, in 1930, and guided here for 40 years.

Now 75, he showed me a video of his last climb up the Grand, five years ago, on the 50th anniversary of his solo ascent and the discovery of a new route, the Exum Ridge. Seeing pictures of the steep climb scared me even more. But Exum had a calming effect, too. He acted as though anybody could climb the Grand Teton. "Like any sport, the key ingredient is desire," he said. "You look in pretty good shape. Give it a go."

The morning of the basic school was sunny and hot. I wore shorts, a T-shirt and running shoes. I was issued a helmet, and I had to sign a paper saying I could die. Then it was off for the Jenny Lake boat with six others and guide Peter Lev, one of Exum's owners. Peter wore a Tyrolean hat, knickers and an old backpack that looked held together with bailing wire. After 26 years of guiding here, he fit like an old shoe.

We learned to walk, we learned to tie ropes around our waist, we learned to keep our eyes on our feet when we climbed, to rivet them to the rock. I was thankful to learn that you don't pull yourself up with your arms. I can only do five and a half pull-ups.

You use your feet and legs. Your hands and arms are hooks and levers. We learned that in spots you push yourself away from the rock, a "layback" so that your feet improve their grip. It looked so easy when Peter did it.

I squirmed over boulder faces that seemed as smooth as a pond, praying for a ripple to dig a fingernail into. I was aware of the hot rock, and sometimes of my heart and lungs, excited. Yet I felt safe. Secured to a belay above — nothing more than a person with a rope wrapped around his waist — I ventured out onto a 45-degree pitch in search of nooks and crannies. I heard Glenn Exum's words in my mind. "Don't fight the mountain. Take your time."

We put our trust in each other, strangers from Illinois and Virginia thrown together in a class. We all had to test the belay, lean away from the rock, hands spread, secured by a half-inch rope that we had tied ourselves around our waists, and held at the other end by a stranger. I belayed a gangling boy from Vancouver who slipped twice, holding him until he regained his composure. I felt as though I had done it all my life.

By the end of the day we rappelled over a small cliff, falling under our own control 25 feet to the rock below. And we could see the eyes of hikers on us, from down at the base of Hidden Falls.

Maybe they were actually watching the class next to us, rappelling 125 feet, climbing what looked like a nearly vertical wall. It was the intermediate class, and before I could climb the Grant Teton — my goal — I had to go through it, too. That would come tomorrow.

JULY 7

- - -

When I turned over in my sleeping bag, I could see the Tetons through the window of the little cabin. I was on a lower bunk, sharing a room with other climbers at the Grand Teton Climbing Ranch. I say "other climbers" because I still felt like an outsider, and I hung back from their talk about "10-A pitches" and "protection." I didn't want to admit that I had just finished "basic."

They were a wiry bunch, steel coils with skin and hair. For $4 a night, they got a bunk and a bath at the foot of the Tetons. Each day they would go out in search of cracks in granite, new mountains to conquer. For them, the Tetons were among the finest in the United States, with "good" rock, that is to say, safe, interesting and scenic. Every year, thousands of these climbers come here.

I slunk off to intermediate class at Exum, hoping I could feel a part, hoping I would pass. I was teamed with a young woman and man who worked at the Grand Teton Lodge, a cop from California and a fellow graduate from my basic class, a well-read, well-meaning New Yorker named Nick who seemed to stumble through life as he stumbled through belays. I didn't trust him with my life.

Our instructor was Chuck Pratt, 47, short and stocky, with a gray beard and the same bald look of Joe Garagiola. Glenn Exum had called Pratt, "a pure guy." His life was rock climbing. He'd dropped out of physics to pioneer in Yosemite, at a time when climbers were thought nuts with death wishes. He'd climbed El Capitan, eating and sleeping while hanging from ropes. He knew what he was doing.

And, from the start of the class at Hidden Falls, he stressed safety. We learned how to protect him as he climbed ahead of us; we learned how to use stoppers and "friends," mechanical devices that slip into cracks for protection, and are removed by the last man up. They largely have replaced pitons, which were driven into rock, but often damaged it. And then we tried bouldering, getting the feel of granite. We used hand jams and foot jams, and whole body jams, if the cracks were wide enough.

"The essence of rock climbing is problem solving for your own body," said Chuck. Good climbers are analytic. It's also like a dance, and ballet dancers make the best climbers, "because they're feet oriented," he said.

After lunch, we roped together and began our first pitch. It was not exactly vertical, but steep enough to strain your neck watching Chuck dance up it, and it was tough from the first move. You balanced on one arm on a small ledge while grasping blindly overhead for a handhold.

Chuck climbed first to a small ledge 25 feet up, yelled "climb" for the next in line, and began the safety belay as the student yelled, "climbing." When we reached Chuck, he belayed the next person in line, and Chuck ascended another pitch. We worked our way up.

There were moments of panic. The holds were slippery from sweaty palms. On the third pitch, 75 feet up, we had to belly to the left over smooth rock, find a handhold and lean back so that our soles could cling. I cheated and used a knee at the top of one ledge, bruising it. One finger bled.

At the top, we sat on the rock and rested, feeling good, feeling safe, wanting beer. The falls foamed to our left, and Jenny Lake spread out in the distance.

To get down, we rappelled 90 feet over a cliff. We were belayed by Chuck, but we controlled our speed on a second rope which passed through a metal figure-8 hooked with a locking carabiner to a crotch harness.

I went too fast. My leather gloves burned. The metal, at the bottom, was too hot to pick up with bare hands. Three blisters welled up on my right hand from rope burns through the cowhide.

And then we did it all again, ascending an "open book" where two walls come together, stretching across pockmarks in the rock, using hand jams and lay-backs, sweating, scaring ourselves.

As I passed one protection device, balanced on two sets of toes and one hand, I tried to clip it into the rope below me. It fell out. My leg began a "sewing machine" shake. I had to go up.

After another rappel we were done. Chuck said I had passed and could climb the Grand Teton tomorrow. So could Nick.

The rock on the intermediate class was rated 5.6 in toughness, he said. The Exum Ridge on the mountain was rated 5.5. We had been put through tougher rocks in school to see if we had the right stuff for the Grand.

JULY 9

- - -

We began our climb of the Grant Teton late in the morning. I
borrowed an old aluminum-framed pack from the Exum Guide
Service and jammed in enough stuff to clothe an army.

The guides insisted on wool: socks, gloves, hat, underwear,
pants, shirts and sweater, as well as a rain jacket, a parka, water,
sunscreen, boots and enough food for two lunches, dinner and
breakfast. I also carried a camera, a tape recorder and notebook.

The 13,700-foot Grand can be climbed in a day. You gain a
mile in altitude, and the hike is 9 miles long; the record up and back
is something like four hours. But Exum does it in two days, climbing
the first day to the lower saddle, just over 11,400 feet, where you eat
and sleep in a tent, ascending the peak early on the second day.

I had planned to climb with a guide, alone, but realized after
two days of class that half the fun of rock climbing is the
camaraderie of the group, our fates roped together, our trust in the
team.

Our group included New Yorker Nick, who took off with the
price tags dangling on his new gear; Mark from Kansas, a building
designer and another beginner; and Bill, a computer consultant from
Vancouver, a veteran of winter climbs and one-time guide. He had
every high-tech device known to man, from striped polypropylene
pants that made him look like Big Bird, to freeze-dried spaghetti in a
bag.

What a contrast to Chuck Pratt, our guide, who wore a burned
pair of corduroys, lived on cheese and mustard, and drank snowmelt.

It wasn't long up the trail before I was breathing heavily, My
pack squeaked. I felt like a mule. By the time we emerged from the
trees into a boulder field and snow, I was wet and the wind felt good.
We soon put on wool pants and parkas.

We crossed a snow field, steep and slushy. Chuck scared me to death with warnings that you can slide out of control into wet holes and drown before someone reaches you. A kid did that last year, and we crossed right above his grave.

We held an ice ax in our uphill hand, roped ourselves 3 feet apart, and crept across, diagonally upward. It reminded me of an Everest ascent. At times the wind threatened to tip us all over. If it did we were to go into "self-arrest," digging our toes and axes into the snow. We crossed maybe 2 miles of snow.

I was tense. I braced for a slip. I watched each step and placed my boots in the footsteps ahead of me. We were mostly silent, except for Nick. When he began reciting the Declaration of Independence, maybe to break his tension, it irritated me.

At the headwall to the saddle, Chuck had to choose between another snow traverse, a slushy stairway to Heaven, and a route over rocks using a rope. He chose the rocks. It was a mistake. The rocks beneath the rope had become a waterfall, and near the top we had to belay across a short, dangerous snow field. It was wet and exhausting.

Eight hours after we started we reached the top of the saddle, home to rocks, a marmot or two and some sturdy wildflowers. The packs fell from our backs. The wind from the west battered us. Chuck estimated it at 50 mph.

The john sat facing Idaho, and it took a strong man to sit there. There was no way to urinate without spraying either yourself or Jackson, Wyo. If you turned your back to the hurricane, it created an enormous eddy which made things worse.

Our home for the night was a large tent stretched over a tubular frame and exposed to the wind. It was like being in a base drum. We sat inside and heated water for soup and coffee.

We stretched out side by side, us five and a family of six, and tried to sleep. Chuck gave up and moved outside. He didn't sleep either.

If I slept, I don't remember. The alarm went off at 3:30. The wind had never stopped. My hope of setting off July 4th fireworks early that morning blew away with the gusts.

I didn't feel like eating. I jammed rock shoes and water into my daypack and a bag of almonds into my pocket. I put on a ski jacket and stumbled out into the wind after Chuck.

By 4:30 we were headed onto a boulder field on our way to the summit. The wing gusted and stopped, and blew again. It knocked me three feet off the trail at times.

I wasn't at all sure I wanted to climb today. But I stumbled on in the dark.

JULY 13

- - -

We began the final ascent of the Grand Teton with baby steps, walking behind Chuck Pratt, our guide, in a series of switchbacks up the lower saddle.

We walked close together without speaking. The wind whistled through our helmets and the stocking caps beneath them. It was dark and cold and the peak was out of sight to the north, 2,200 feet up.

I walked behind Chuck. Behind me I could hear the clink of a carabiner on a harness Mark had slung over his shoulder. He and Nick, the next in line, carried our ropes, two 150-foot lengths of 7-16th-inch nylon. Bill walked last.

The rocks grew in size. We could kick them over when we started. Within an hour they were the side of bedrooms. We crawled through the "Eye of the Needle," a cave formed by several boulders. That's when the real climb began.

Behind us a family of two men and three boys was starting out. They had spent the night in the tent, too, but were taking a different route, the Owen-Spaulding route by which the Grand was first climbed in 1898.

Last year 1,804 people climbed the Grand, 534 of them guided, on 20 some routes. Five people died climbing in the Tetons last year, six the year before.

"Nobody better fall," Chuck said as we finished our first belay and began another scramble through the boulders.

When we weren't climbing, we walked "in coils," tied together at the waist, the spare rope coiled in one hand as we struggled to keep up.

It was 6:20 a.m. and we were still in shadow as we hit Wall Street, the first landmark of the Exum Ridge. The "street" lies against a sheer wall, narrowing to a point at which you must either jump eight feet over a 1,500-foot chasm or hang by your fingers and toes and inch around, your butt hanging out in the wind. Glenn Exum jumped in 1931, when he found the route, but no one has done it since. It is a place of enormous exposure, where even the guide must be protected with a belay.

I braced myself and played the rope from my waist as Chuck hung over the edge and disappeared. I tried to memorize where he placed his feet and hands. In too short a time he was yelling to me, "Climb."

I didn't want to look down. Even looking up was dizzying because of clouds that streaked overhead. I tried to watch my hands and my feet. Yet the chasm would sneak in on the edge. The rock was cold. I wore leather gloves and rock shoes, tight, ballet-like lace-ups with no edge to their sticky rubber soles.

When Chuck's face peered over, I smiled. I took over the belay, as he clambered up the next pitch, the Golden Staircase, into the sun. I couldn't watch his feet; I was busy with Mark.

It wasn't a bad climb, except for the wind, which pummeled my body and filled my helmet, vibrating it against my head. My collar flapped against my glasses. I didn't need the distraction.

Climbing focuses you. Nothing else matters but that next handhold. Even roped you are terribly alone, just you and the rock to which you cling, from which you seek a hold on life. For me the worst was mid-belay on the "Friction Pitch," out of sight of Chuck and the team I left behind.

The wind threatened to rip me away. I would feel a tingle and recognize the panic, rising to grip my muscles, to freeze me, exposed and helpless. It was an old feeling, from my childhood, when I tried to climb a wet glen and nearly slipped to a foolish death.

I would drive it away, time and again, by sheer concentration on the rock, the steps, each so tiny, but better than the enormity of what I was doing. In this way I inched my way up.

After six or eight belays I asked for rest. We slumped on a small ridge and drank water. I was queasy. Mark asked what I was thinking. "How much more?" And Chuck said, "We're half way." He got us moving quickly.

On the mountain there was no sense of progress, save one — we walked on exposed slopes next to dropoffs as if we were mountain goats, not rank beginners. Each pitch led to another. We could not see the summit. The walls and boulders surrounded and diminished us.

When Chuck told us we had made the last belay, we practically ran the long scramble through a boulder field to the top.

I whooped. I stood on the geologic survey marker and made Vs with my fingers. We took pictures until we ran out of film. I tried to think of something significant to say — it being the 4th of July and all — but all that came was another whoop.

We signed the register, rolled in a tube, and looked for a long time at Jackson Hole below. In an odd way, the peak was anticlimactic. The view was like that from an airplane.

Chuck admitted he had never seen the wind so bad. Later we learned it had been 60 mph. A boy in the family behind us suffered hypothermia and was rushed down before he could sign the register.

Bill asked if I felt macho. I didn't. I felt humble and proud. Nick said it had changed his life. Being at the top of the mountain wasn't important. Getting there was.

JULY 16

- - -

I must tell you that for this aging body, climbing the Grand Teton was mind over matter. I felt it nearly everywhere the next day.

The worst part was the nine miles down. Descents are dangerous, because you're tired. We made two long rappels and reached the base tent about lunchtime. The tent was still banging in the wind. I was glad to be done with ropes.

Then began the long walk across the snow fields — just as dangerous — through the boulders, down the path to the car. We arrived about 6 p.m. I've never been as tired. I treated myself to the last room available in Jackson on July 4, took a bath, fell asleep and never heard the fireworks outside.

All I remember about the next morning was groans. If I lifted my head, it hurt. If I raised my arm, it ached. If I tried to sit up, even the groan hurt.

But boy did I feel good inside.

It was a beautiful, brisk day. A storm had moved through, dropping two inches of snow on the lower saddle, where we had stayed the night before. The temperature had dipped to 19 up there. I drove back to Jenny Lake, bought a couple of T-shirts at the Exum Guide Service and stopped to look at the Teton range. A cloud covered the Grand. I couldn't see where I had been, or what I had done. But it was all inside. I turned on the radio real loud and took off for Yellowstone. For once, even the traffic didn't bother me.

Driving alone, I tried out words, aloud, to describe my feelings. Maybe it was the holiday, but soon I was saying things about patriotism and the American way. We had climbed as a team, the five of us, and put our lives in each other's hands. Yet our goals had been private, the victories personal.

I drove past families at roadside picnic tables and men in waders, fishing the streams. These people, like us on the mountain, were expressing their individuality, their freedom to choose — even if it was a picnic spot or a trout pool.

Suddenly, Yellowstone came to mean all that. In the flush of the moment, I began to think of this park as the repository of things American.

It is a place where we can be free: free from the telephone, free to climb a mountain, free from structure, free to fish, free from urban noise, free to cook on a campfire, free from the clock, free to do nothing. True, there are rules and regulations. But I couldn't help thinking, as I drove home to my cabin, that freedom runs as a thread in this park. People enjoy it in many different ways.

I think it was Ron Blanchard, a river runner, who told me, "Yellowstone is essentially an individual's park."

What could be more American than that?

JULY 18

- - -

The story on the news could have been just another death, just another accident in a national park. But this one I could feel. I had been there.

Abigail Mackey, a 21-year-old summer employee at Yellowstone, had slid to her death on Skillet Glacier in the Tetons while climbing with friends earlier this week. Not too many days before, I had crossed a snowfield south of there while climbing the Grand Teton. I had seen then what could happen, what did happen to her. And it scared me as much as anything on the mountain.

But I made it, thanks to a good guide, good training and luck. As I considered her mistake — no helmet, no rope, the wrong path — there was little to be smug about. It could have been me.

Every year in Yellowstone country, people die needlessly. They make mistakes, misjudge, forget. In Yellowstone park last year, 10 people died accidentally — four drownings, two car accidents, two hiking falls, one poisoning (a man ate water hemlock), and one suffocation. There also were seven heart attacks, considered natural deaths, and one homicide.

In 1984, there were two accidental deaths, a drowning and a bear attack. The year before, a Frenchman was fatally gored by a buffalo while his friends took his picture. It's also rare that someone isn't burned, at least injured, by a thermal pool.

By any measure, death here can be exotic. Boiled alive. Eaten by a bear. It's the nature of this place to be exotic. If it weren't there would be no park.

Yet, lulled by inns and paved campsites, it's easy to forget that this is a wild place, that the animals by the road are untamed, that the pretty lake with its boats is a killer. Yellowstone is not a city park. There is a certain risk just in coming.

59

"Many forget where they are," said Curt Menefee, a Denver-based park attorney. "People come for vacation. They relax their guard. What better place than a national park? It's probably the worst place. They not only leave their cares behind. They leave their common sense, too."

As a result, park managers spend an enormous amount of time and money trying to protect people from the park. But how far should they go? Do they line the canyon with guardrails? Do they pave the paths? One woman who turned her ankle argued in federal court that the park should sweep the rocks away. Fortunately, she lost.

Courts have accepted the argument that parks exist to preserve wilderness, and that bears, hot pools and falling trees are natural occurrences. Legal success often rides, however, on whether the park has adequately warned visitors of dangers. After an accident, rangers scurry around taking pictures of signs, detailing warnings people received. On evening patrols, every cooler seen, every oral warning given, is put in a report.

A couple of years ago, visitors were handed a pamphlet that was almost cutesy, with cartoon bears standing over a camper with a hotdog and little devils stoking the thermal areas. The newer pamphlet is scarier, the drawings realistic. After 12 gorings last summer, a special pamphlet was rushed out showing a man being thrown into the air by a bison.

Interestingly, in the Tetons, where the danger is so evident, climbing lawsuits are rare. As Ed Christian, the Teton assistant chief ranger said, "We can't make people do anything. There's no way to test skills, there's no way to test equipment. They are told of hazards. Most are very aware. They just go out and take their chances. They are out there on nature's terms."

JULY 20

- - -

It felt like fall today. I baked bread last night as a thunderstorm
rolled through, and toasted it this morning to chase the chill.

The campers outside the cabin all wore sweatshirts. Not until
mid-afternoon was it warm enough for T-shirts.

The night before last, I went back to Fishing Bridge and poked
around with ranger Jeff Henry. We looked for signs of grizzly bears.
Two hundred yards from the RV park, near Pelican Creek, he took
me to the bones and skin of an elk calf, partially buried by a grizzly.
The carcass was relatively fresh and smelled.

Down on the shore of Yellowstone Lake, a stone's throw from
the campground, the breakers were coming hard, pushed by cold
winds. Jeff saw a faint paw print in the sand, but said it was
impossible to tell how old it was. If there were others, they had been
wiped out by the surf or the footprints of humans, which were
plentiful.

At Fishing Bridge, as nowhere else in Yellowstone, man and
bear meet. It is a place of continuing conflict, a place both enjoy and
frequent. It is also a scrimmage line blurred by the footprints of
rhetoric.

Fishing Bridge is the nicest campground in the park, near the
water, with lots of trees and space. The visitor center and the
Hamilton Store are beautiful old buildings from the 1920s. Even the
rundown garage, its doors sagging on a tree-trunk frame, has a
certain charm.

For 50 years, people dropped their lines from the bridge that
crossed the Yellowstone River to catch cutthroat trout — thus, the
name Fishing Bridge. To protect the fish, the park stopped that
practice in 1973.

To protect the bear, it proposed closing the whole complex, and
began tearing down cabins. The campground and RV park were to be

closed by this year. But the public objected — the RV lobby, concession operators, and Cody, the town closest to Fishing Bridge. The result was political intervention, a new study, protests, arrests, a lawsuit — and business as usual this year at Fishing Bridge.

I don't know who to believe.

The park argues, with enough justification to fill a book, that Fishing Bridge jeopardizes the grizzly bear's future in Yellowstone. There have been too many conflicts with man and too many bears killed as a result.

On the other hand, the park has hurt its credibility by building Grant Village, also on Yellowstone Lake, in grizzly habitat. It is considered a substitute for Fishing Bridge, but just as many bears have been removed from there as from Fishing Bridge, and the park may someday have to block spawning trout in nearby streams to keep bears away.

Because of the danger of bears and man meeting in the Fishing Bridge campground, the park closed the loop closest to Pelican Creek this year. But if you stand there by the empty picnic tables, as I did, and pace off the distance to the picnic tables in the next open loop, you see how ridiculous is this compromise. No hungry bear would let 15 paces stop him.

All of which is not lost on campers, who feel the park is trying to exclude them and is using the bear to justify it.

I'm not much for conspiracy theories, but there is certainly a rigidity to the arguments here. Watching the park rangers haul environmental protesters off the bridge is proof enough of that. The bear is lost in the shouting.

One thing I know for sure: Fishing Bridge is as good an example as any of Yellowstone's basic design flaw — an attempt to compromise between man and nature. Drawing the line is an art, not so much in biology as in diplomacy.

JULY 22

- - -

I first heard the boys from Germany in song, sitting on a picnic table in the sun, bellowing something from their homeland. I offered them a beer.

"Beer? Yes? Why not!" And they laughed.

Gerd Grau and Ulrich Fischbach had just spent two days in Yellowstone, discovering one of its awful truths.

"It's all arranged by car," said Gerd, 24. "It's not easy for hikers," said Ulrich, 23. "There are no trailheads near the camps. You need a car to get to the trailheads. It is…" and they conferred in German a minute, "anti-hiker."

They had come to be thrilled — "We don't have geysers in Germany. We don't have buffaloes in Germany."

It pained me that they had missed so much.

"In the campground it was a little bit boring to me," said Ulrich, unshaven, with long blond hair. "I wanted to see wildlife. Lots of Americans told me Yellowstone would be very nice."

They had hitched from West Yellowstone to the Madison campground and from there to the geyser basin; it had taken two days.

"In Scotland," he said, "there is not much traffic. If a car passes by and there is a place for us, it stops for sure. In Ireland, too, it is easy, if you're not English."

In the United States they found the easiest hitching on the Blackfeet Indian Reservation in Montana. In the park, most rides came from employees, not fellow tourists.

"A couple of miles from camp, there are trailers passing by. They act like turning — shaking — their heads. Some hours later you see this guy in the restroom and he's very friendly. 'Hi, how are you today?' He's very friendly. But not on that road."

"It should be possible," said Ulrich, "to take this loop in seven days by bus, and get on and off, and tell the driver, 'Please pick me up in three days, at 9 o'clock.'"

In Germany they were workers, Gerd a rugged, blond apprentice in what he translated as "central heating" and Ulrich a taxi-driver waiting for a spot in "forest economics" college. He spoke English well. At home, he gave rides to many American GIs who didn't talk much — "They want a fast ride to Wendy's or McDonald's."

They were fascinated with the motor homes that passed them by in the park.

"How do they…are they normally workers, or do they own factories?" asked Ulrich.

"Sometimes," said Gerd, "I see not just motor homes. I see ships. I see them pulling a car, with a motorcycle and bicycle. Can the normally worker afford that, and a boat, too?"

"They country is very spectacular," said Ulrich. "They national parks are very beautiful. I like this country. If we thought about the politics and the president, there is no reason to come to the U.S.," he said. "In Germany there are a lot of young people working to get the cruise missiles out."

"But we don't come to America to want to make politics," said Gerd. "We don't have a national park. We have national forests, but to see animals, they are arranged in paddocks.

"At home the biggest animal is a fox. We have no moose and bears. There's so much to see."

JULY 25

- - -

Dick Crysdale and his gang drove all night from Denver to begin their Yellowstone vacation, hauling two canoes behind a Wagoneer stuffed to the gills.

When I met them, the canoes already were afloat by the Grant Village breakwater and piled high with coolers and plastic bags. They looked more like garbage scows bound for the dump than for a wilderness trip.

It was 20 miles to the south arm of Yellowstone Lake, where they planned to camp, and they wanted an early start, before the lake came to life with wind and waves.

Dick and his buddy, Don Son, had known the lake since the 1950s, when they were fishing guides. So they knew about one of Yellowstone's best-kept secrets — the lakeshore campsites at the southern tips, off-limits to motors, rarely used, a water wilderness where the cutthroat trout practically throw themselves into your frying pan.

But first came the red tape. It took an hour to get the backcountry permits. They could stay three nights at any one campsite, so a week's vacation meant three moves. The rules changed annually, they said. One year, they moved camp every night.

They filled out forms. They watched a slide show, got a short lecture, paid a $10 fee for each boat and then filled out more paperwork, saying they had been briefed. I could see their temperature rising as the sun rose. By the time they fired up small motors on their square-stern canoes, the lake had a small chop and Dick was fired up.

"The lake is over-regulated," he said. "It discourages people."

When we stopped at Plover Point to stretch our legs and a boat ranger ran us off, Dick said the guy should be fired.

As we motored down the South Arm at 5 mph and passed a few boats bobbing at the shoreline, Dick looked pained. "This is the most number of people I've seen in the arm in 15 years. Everywhere I look!"

I had met Dick Crysdale by mail, after these letters started in The Post. He wrote me long, impassioned pleas for Yellowstone, by hand, on lined note paper. He called the park a "Messiah — Yellowstone is to land management and use as Christ is to Christianity. Yellowstone is older and more symbolic of the United States than the Statue of Liberty. Both symbolize freedom, the statue for people and Yellowstone for wildlife."

He urged me to "sensitize" myself to Yellowstone, to provoke readers to the dangers of Yellowstone's demise. The park, he wrote, receives numerous requests to install TV relay stations, develop the gold, use thermal features for energy, harvest timber, hunt game, build roads around the lake or dams for irrigation.

"Would you let them do it?" he asked me. "Are we a nation so rich we can afford to throw these precious resources away? Or a nation so poor we must sacrifice these precious gems?"

Frankly, his letters disturbed me. He wanted me to feel his fervor, to rail against forces at work against the park.

It was difficult enough just to write myself into the letters, to use the word "I." I had spent a lifetime trying to be an objective journalist, to report without judgement.

But when Dick offered to take me into his paradise, I jumped at the chance. I wanted to hear his opinion firsthand. Here was a park outsider, but one who knew and loved Yellowstone.

He was tall, gray-haired, athletic with a slight paunch from too much desk duty, and a lover of wilderness. I could see him relax as we began paddling the last three miles of the arm, into the non-motor zone.

Dick had brought his stepson, Mark Norgard, on his first trip to Yellowstone. And Don brought his nephew from Missouri, Larry Johnson.

About 1 o'clock, we nosed into a small bay at the tip of the arm, alarming a flock of Golden Eye, which took off, their wings squeaking almost mechanically.

We unloaded the canoes. I counted 30 plastic bags, two big ice chests, a case of pop, tents, Tupperware filled with Wonder Bread, gas cans, rope, Coleman fuel, a folding table, tents, sleeping bags, rod cases and tackle boxes.

We set up a food tent, broke out the Wonder Bread, Miracle Whip, Tato Skins, cold meat, cheese, lettuce and double-stuffed Oreo Cookies, and ate as though it was our last supper. It was only lunch.

JULY 27

\- - -

We fished for our supper, the first night in the back country. Using hammered brass lures, the trout wouldn't leave us alone, and we fried them in corn meal until we couldn't eat anymore.

Dick Crysdale had offered to share his tent with me, a lightweight, white and blue dome made of material a friend used to call waterproof smoke. We set it up on a grassy knoll not far from the water, but a long way from the food tent.

We were in grizzly country. There was scat everywhere, and the backcountry office had warned us not to venture away from the shoreline.

We stored the coolers and food on slings pulled high on a bear bar, a branch hung between two trees. Dick and Don Son had put the bars up on earlier trips to the south arm of Yellowstone Lake, but in 15 years they never had seen a bear.

They had known the lake before regulation, when motorboats were allowed anywhere, when night crawlers were bait and you could take five fish over 14 inches.

As fishing guides, they had argued against a nonmotor wilderness area. But now they loved it because there were so few people around. Last year just under 500 people in 100 watercraft used the seven campsites in the south arm. It was so isolated, so unused, that you began to think of yourself as alone, and the sight of another canoe disturbing.

I was surprised at how noisy it was. Ducks and geese honking, loons laughing, the beating of wings, the splashing of moose through bogs, cries of animals we couldn't identify, the crash of things in the woods, even thunder and rain as I'd never heard it before. "The symphony of nature," Dick called it.

In my reverie I even began to look on the thick lodgepole stands at the water's edge as pipes on a natural organ. Except where man had cleaned a campsite, the shoreline was a jumbled mess. Man left a circle of rocks for fire, and a square of logs around it. In wilderness, a few feet away, there was random order.

Where man had stood, the earth was hard and "clean." Elsewhere it was moist and spongy, with colors of green and brown and gray, of life and decay together. When I dropped a white tissue there, it jarred.

Over the three days that I spent with Dick, we talked a lot about wilderness and the park's attempt to regulate it. I found my early impression of his views changing.

"Wilderness is a concept between the ears," he said. "Wilderness is doing what you want when you want it. It's frustrating to go through the Mickey Mouse. We had freedom in here before."

Ironically, he said, "you get your freedom through regulation. Otherwise the place would be overrun by boats."

He waved at the scene before us. "I could say everybody should see this, but then I wouldn't enjoy it. This is really wonderful, and it's all because of the screwy regulations."

Yellowstone, as it turned out, had been the cradle of Dick Crysdale's career. As a guide he had met Laurence Rockefeller, who was recommending to President Kennedy the creation of a Bureau of Outdoor Recreation.

After four years as a boat ranger on Yellowstone, Dick got his master's in recreation, writing his thesis on the zoning of Yellowstone Lake. He then went to work for the new bureau. Eventually he became an outdoor recreation planner for the Bureau of Reclamation, responsible for 291 projects in 17 western states.

The bureau, the bad guys of big government, allowed all manner of motorized toys on their land.

"The bureau lands are playgrounds, whereas this is a museum," Dick said. "We sacrifice some lands to preserve places like this. We take a lot of pressure off of national parks. The national parks are successful in staving off development, so that when my kids are grown up they can come here and see the same thing I've seen here over the last 30 years.

"The parks are kinda like an attic for the nation. We really haven't discovered what we have here. But we are constantly asking questions about where we came from and how we relate to the environment. Here they can see what our ancestors and the pioneers encountered.

"If the park service didn't take an ultra-conservative position, we couldn't have what we have now."

I took a canoe out by myself, to practice my casting, to take some pictures, to listen more to the symphony. I tried to dip the oar so as not the bang the aluminum canoe — it echoed across the lake when I slipped.

In the quiet, several hundred yards offshore, I heard a new sound, a deep, rhythmic rumbling from somewhere near our camp. Only after I beached did I find the source.

Dick Crysdale, in the sleeping bag next to mine, snoring.

AUGUST

AUGUST 1

\- - -

It was nearing midnight as John Railey checked his watch by the light of a small flashlight, set his stopwatch and listened again for the famous gush.

We were not alone. Around the geyser, dark figures stood, shivering, waiting for one last eruption before bed. Some, close enough to hear, listed as Railey explained how he predicts the intervals between eruptions.

"If it's a short eruption following a long, then I predict 53 minutes. If a long following a short, 80. If a long following a long, 76. If it's a rare three-minute burst, then 65."

The geyser spit a little, and we turned our heads in that direction.

"Some people think we turn it off at night," said Railey. We all laughed, and Old Faithful erupted again.

For 10 summers, John Railey has been keeping tabs on Old Faithful, as faithful a "geyser gazer" as they come. From 8 p.m., when the visitor center closes, until 1 or 2 in the morning, Railey checks each eruption, notes it carefully in a log and predicts the next one. At night you can see him in there, hunched over a calculator, his glasses and bald head showing above his green volunteer jacket.

After he retires to his room at the Old Faithful Inn, an infrared detector on the roof records each hot spray and scratches it on a graph.

The next night Railey catches up with the statistics that allow geyser geologist Rick Hutchinson to say: "Old Faithful is still faithful, but on its own schedule. It's still predictable, its maximum height is still 40 meters. It never was once an hour, on the hour."

After Old Faithful spouted, Railey led the way to his office and showed me a printout of the intervals this year. In the first five months, it has ranged from 41 minutes to 106 minutes. The historic range is 33 minutes to 120 minutes.

The "average" used to be 65 minutes, giving rise, I suppose, to the once-an-hour tale. But in fact, Hutchinson said, Old Faithful always has been variable.

Earthquakes in 1959 and 1983 boosted the average — and began the rumor that Old Faithful was dying or unfaithful. The average went to 78 minutes after the last quake. The current average is 72.4, but the range is still wide. While I was there it was 45 minutes and 80-some, but still fairly close to the prediction.

I think that's why Old Faithful is so popular — it fits the American preoccupation with time. A tourist on a tight schedule can rush up, park in the big ugly parking lot that used to be a campground, walk a few yards, check the electronic tote board for the next eruption, catch the show and leave. Many people do just that.

It's the worst way to see, or remember, Yellowstone. It's also the kind of action that offends Railey and his fellow geyser gazers — people caught by the magic of the geyser field who spend their summers, or vacations, watching. People whose strongest attribute is patience.

One summer recently, a young married woman Railey knows caught 100 consecutive eruptions of the Grand Geyser, which erupts every nine hours.

Railey, retired as a Los Angeles draftsman in 1977, likes to watch the Grand, too, just like any tourist, although it's difficult for him to walk the distance to the geyser and climb the steps without handrails.

But it's Old Faithful that he is most loyal to, and most protective of — the reason he spends his summer here, at his own expense, watching and calculating.

"I'm looking for something to do," he says.

I suspect it's something more than that.

AUGUST 3

\- - -

Yellowstone at night is a wilderness of the mind, where all that you have seen takes new shape in your imagination. Especially in a geyser area.

My daughter and I walked at midnight through the upper geyser basin, armed with a flashlight and the memory of a daytime walk. We tromped down the boardwalk, passing noises and smells new to us. Our glasses steamed over. Our minds went wild.

"Promise you won't laugh if I tell you the truth?" Amy said. She took my hand.

"Yes."

"I'm scared."

"Me too."

We stood at the maw of the Giant Geyser and turned off our light. It roared unspeakable fury from somewhere far below. If licks of flame had appeared, I would not have been surprised.

"Wouldn't it be cool to see down inside?" she said.

"You want to try it?"

"No! Don't, Dad."

The geysers of Yellowstone are often described in diabolic, infernal terms. Unworldly is a common one. I think just the opposite. To me the geysers speak most articulately of an earth alive. A living planet. Where else in the world, except for rare eruptions, can you sense that? They also make Yellowstone a place of constant change and surprise.

Last year, Excelsior geyser, the biggest in the park, erupted for the first time in 95 years in a 47-hour display that brought geyser researcher Rick Hutchinson running. This year, two new geysers erupted. One of them, Fantail, is only 150 yards from the road. Now, the Norris geyser basin is showing signs of an impending major disturbance. Most geology looks at the geologic history, Hutchinson said. Here it changes.

Hutchinson took Amy and me to an unmarked spring in the Norris area, where water is flooding in new places, killing trees. The next day he invited us to walk two hours to another unnamed area where a new mud volcano was throwing hot clay into the trees.

"I get here a sense of the sheer power that's around us," he said, "that makes everything that man has, or thinks he has, pale by comparison."

Hutchinson is a serious researcher, seeking answers to what is going on here. He has studied, for example, silica-encrusted algae and bacteria that point south — they are photosynthetic. He also has found fossil remains of such growth. They also point south. An older deposit might give scientists clues to the movement of the earth's surface if, for example, such fossils point east.

But Hutchinson also just enjoys a good show. One afternoon he sat with the crowd at Echinus and watched the pool fill up, then begin to bubble, and finally dance and spray. Afterward he gave an impromptu talk on the geyser's personality.

"I'm able to do original research, to answer questions for people, to understand the Yellowstone thermal features and to protect them so that Amy can come back with her grandkids to enjoy as much as I am."

Hutchinson, hairy and small with wet eyes and a way with children, speaks with a quiet rage about vandalism at Yellowstone.

"If you can think of something that can be thrown into a geyser, it has been — cement signs, furniture, bottles, clothing."

Park history is rotten with stories of features gone bad because of such trashing. Ebony geyser was once a tall, extremely beautiful geyser, he said. It doesn't erupt anymore because of sticks and rocks that people threw in. Every year Hutchinson cleans bottles and pop and beer cans and rocks and sticks from Old Faithful.

The famous Morning Glory Pool, shaped and colored like a flower, is changing colors because of stuff thrown into it. In 1944, the pool erupted — threw up, really, tossing a pair of underwear, bottles, cans and rocks.

In 1950, Morning Glory was induced to disgorge by draining it. It yielded 76 handkerchiefs, towels and socks, $86.27 in pennies and $8.10 in nickels. There also were tax tokens, 50 percent of which came from the state of Washington.

Amy and I saw fresh pennies thrown into Morning Glory on our daytime walk. At night, though, the pool was colorless. We were left only with sounds. After a time, it no longer seemed scary. We heard water trickling everywhere, soft bubbling liquid, deep dark dollops from holes to nowhere, and the roar of the Lion geyser.

Brave now, we turned off the light and walked in the dark and stood for long moments to drink it in.

"I'm glad we did this," said Amy, her hand now free.

So was I.

AUGUST 6

- - -

The park is at its peak now. The popular campgrounds are full at noon, the hotels and cabins are reserved, and the benches at Old Faithful are covered for the midday shows. Officially, the numbers are up four percent from last year, a far cry from the 40 percent predicted when I arrived in May.

At the souvenir shops, business is good. There is a compulsion to spend money here — to buy something to take home, to give grandma, or the grandkids, or the neighbor keeping the dog.

Many places still call them "curios," short for curiosities and derived, I suppose, from the days when pieces of Yellowstone, antlers, geyserites, petrified wood, you name it, were stolen or sold to visitors. Today they have to settle for items made elsewhere with "Yellowstone" stuck on them.

One afternoon I watched the crowd at Old Faithful stream away from the show toward the Hamilton Store. It's an hourly gold rush for this third-generation family business, the company has the monopoly on things labeled "Yellowstone."

They sell 500 T-shirts a day at their 16 stores, 1,000 rolls of film, 2,500 meals, 500 bags of ice and two dozen bear-shaped bells. They won't say how much they make, but they pay 2-1/2 percent of their gross to the park for the privilege.

Charles Hamilton opened his first store at Old Faithful in 1915. The building is still open, the one with the burl wood sign down the walk from the inn. It's a cozy little place, where the 50 employees (senior citizens or college kids) make $3.50 an hour peddling thousands of items.

Upstairs are dorm rooms and Hamilton's original office, plastered with $1.8 million in canceled checks. He died here in 1957, and they say his ghost still moves about.

Downstairs, in the center of the building, sits a counter just the right height for little boys. Crammed in it are knives and holsters and toothpick holders and little spoons and a million things with bears on them.

Just a stop away is a glass case containing a $41,480 Hopi squash blossom necklace. Fifteen steps away is a Christmas tree with $4 ornaments that sell like ice cream cones on a hot day. A new item in that store this year is a Dickens-like "house" in a winter scene, with a light inside and little sleighs and carolers. The houses are $175 apiece. There's nothing Yellowstone about it.

Behind the counter, in the window, is a Russian cup and saucer, which occasionally brings an indignant remark from a patriot.

The park dictates what Hamilton can sell and the price. Prices must be comparable to stores outside the park — T-shirt markups 100 percent, toys 82 percent, toiletries 69 percent. And the item must somehow be "appropriate." Three times a year, park inspectors check to see that they are.

According to Hamilton employees, the park has rejected Playboy, postcards showing people feeding bears, and T-shirts reading, "I slept with Old Faithful."

Terry Povah, Hamilton's grandson who now heads the company, rails at the park's dictates and predicts that ultimately the park will take over the business and hire a company to manage it.

That's what the park did with the hotels and other concessions. TW Services runs them and pays the park 22 percent of the gross for capital improvements — a deal that has brought in $14 million since 1980s.

By the way, I left the store with a Christmas bell for my mother, a magnetic bear for a refrigerator door, L.L. Bean's fly fishing book, and six teddy bear postcards. I came close to getting the big furry slippers that look like bear feet — but I didn't know her shoe size.

AUGUST 8

- - -

Mecca is a strange term for West Yellowstone, Mont. -- unless you're a fly fisherman and know that the sanctuary lies outside of town, away from the t-shirt shops and cheap motels.

The pilgrims stop to eat and sleep and resupply their worship robes, but they do not stay. Each day they scatter in search of solitude, places of meditation, the perfect water, the perfect cast, the perfect fish.

Not until the 1930s and the coming of the automobile did West Yellowstone become a place known for its fly fishing. Today it is the world center. There are five shops that cater exclusively to fly fishers — as many outlets as there are churches or bars in this town of 756. In addition, there are fly fishing schools, a fly fishing museum, and the international office of the Federation of Fly Fishers.

But the real draw is what they call "blue-ribbon" water, thousands of miles of streams within 150 miles of West Yellowstone that flow clear and sparkling and alive with trout. Here, they say, is the best fishing in the world, much of it in Yellowstone National Park, some of it as good as it ever was.

It got that way, ironically, by the heavy hand of man, by restricting the fishing.

Along the Yellowstone River, thousands of people happily catch and release cutthroat, bending the barbs down on their hooks to reduce injury to the fish.

The biggest complaint on Yellowstone Lake, where you are allowed to keep two fish a day under 13 inches, is that the fish are too big! "What kind of complaint is that?" laughed Ron Jones of the U.S. Fish and Wildlife Service.

Last year a Livingston, Mont. fishing group even gave its annual award to the park. Imagine, the park doing something right.

All of this has come about within the past 25 years, a period of sweeping philosophical change in fishing, led by fishermen.

Streams and lakes here once were stocked with factory-raised fish so that fishermen could harvest them. The park had a hatchery from 1899 to the 1950s. But stocked fish died, didn't reproduce well, didn't fight like wild fish, and didn't taste as good. And there was terrible waste.

I have heard stories of people caught canning hundreds of fish in an RV pulled up alongside park waters. At one time, garbage cans at Fishing Bridge were filled to overflowing with big, unwanted fish.

So they stopped stocking. The result was astounding. Fish got bigger and they were more fun — that is, harder — to catch.

"The meaning of quality fishing changed," said Jones. "Back then, quality was 10 fish on a grill. Today quality is fishing a wild species in a beautiful setting."

The park's first priority now, said Jones, is a healthy trout population and enough for the food chain, which includes bears, eagles and ospreys. The last priority is the fisherman's grill.

Yet cutthroat are easy to catch. One study found that a given cutthroat is caught 10 times a year in the Yellowstone River. The average angler is the park catches one fish an hour. Last year, 160,000 free fishing permits were given out, making these waters some of the most heavily fished in the world.

If everyone who fished Yellowstone Lake were allowed to keep one large fish, however, the fish population would decline to the level of the 1950s, when fishing was said to have collapsed. That's how tenuous is the balance.

"We're not providing a lot of meat," said Bob Gresswell, a fish biologist. "We're providing high quality recreation."

AUGUST 10

- - -

I finally got my feet wet fly fishing.

I was pushed in, really, by my boss, who led me by the arm to a fishing shop and ordered me to make a commitment. He tied his own ties, had a closet full of equipment and, I suspect, wanted to fish the waters of Yellowstone with me.

My reluctance, I think, stemmed from ignorance. It all looked so complicated. There was a uniform, waders and boots and a vest stuffed with enough lines and tools to perform a heart transplant.

Then there were the flies — imitation bugs, thousands of them, it seemed, that the fisherman chose with the care of an entomologist.

I heard of one fanatic who cut open a fish, looked at the bugs inside and proceeded to tie imitations right by the water. Another one told me she pumped a fish's stomach to choose her weapon.

I just wanted to catch a fish, not earn another degree.

I bought a beginner's outfit for $100 that included a long black whip called a graphite rod, a reel, and a fat yellow line I thought sure the fish would see. I also bought a magazine that had stuff in it about knots and casting.

From rows of boxes filled with flies, the clerk helped me pick out several — an elk hair caddis, a leech pattern, a couple of nymphs. By the time he closed the box, I had forgotten which was which.

In the bow of a canoe, it didn't seem the matter. The guys with me were catching fish right and left, using triple-hooked metal lures and spinning rods. I chose a big ugly thing and opened the magazine to knots.

In short order, they had their supper in the boat, the magazine was soaked, and I had caught everything in sight except fish — the bow, my shirt, every other line in the boat. I was suddenly aware that here in this Garden of Eden with my fly rod, I was going to starve to death.

Thank God people took pity on me.

First, somebody caught my supper.

Then, back in West Yellowstone, Maggie Merriman showed me how to cast. She took me into the old railroad depot, now a beautiful fly-fishing museum, and out of the wind worked on my technique.

"The purpose of casting is control of the line," she said, "to get the line, leader and fly out to where the fish are."

She worked with a clock, with a folding rule, with music, with a rod strung with pink yarn, and, finally, with my rod. She taught me how to look forward and backward, to correct my own errors.

"Casting is visual. Fishing is visual," she said. You watch the fly, and when the fish strikes, you lift the rod to see the hook in its mouth. Unlike the old bobber and worm days of my youth, this took concentration.

Maggie also preached simplicity — she had fished for years without waders and a vest. She made a list of stuff I could carry in my shirt pocket.

Next, a fellow from Aurora, Tom Vitolo, wrote and offered to take me fishing in his boat on the Yellowstone River. Tom had fly-fished 20 years, and as we floated, he put the boat within easy shot of the quiet, shady spots along shore. My job was to lay the fly in there, imitating a real bug landing on the water, and let it drift, naturally.

On my sixth cast I caught one. Tom jumped out of the boat and netted it. He also took my picture — except the fish was almost hidden by my hand.

I worked hard the rest of the day, trying to imitate nature without much luck. But I began to understand the lure of fly fishing. It's a problem-solving sport. I was so engrossed in that fly that I didn't think of anything else — not even the gorgeous scenery drifting by.

"It's an intellectual pursuit," said Mike Brady, a guide at Mike Lilly's Trout Shop.

The sport has an elitist reputation. It began with the gentry of England, and in this country, with wealthy members of fishing clubs. Today, fly fishermen still only represent 10 percent of the fishing public.

Just for the fun of it, I stopped one day along the Yellowstone River and asked the first 10 fly fishermen their occupation.

In order: doctor, physician's assistant, college professor, physicist, secretary (with the physicist), photographer, high school senior, electronic technician, research chemist and chemical engineer.

The physicist, somewhat defensive, suggested my sample was biased. Compared to other places, he said, it takes money and time to come to Yellowstone to fly fish.

Incidentally, the boss and I did fish the park without much luck. Our first day out on the Yellowstone, I caught a 20-foot pine tree behind me. The boss, not to be outdone, hooked a 25-footer.

AUGUST 15

- - -

The night that park ranger Mona Divine took me on road patrol was pretty normal for Yellowstone.

She checked a trumpeter swan nest, looked for a bear, posed for a picture with a tourist, woke up a camper who had left a cooler outside, and watched for escaped game-warden killer Clyde Dallas Jr., whose car was found in the park.

It turned out, days later, that the car belonged to someone else, but the report illustrated aptly the rude shove of the outside world into this sanctuary of sanity.

Divine, her long hair tucked beneath her Stetson, wore a .357 Magnum on her hip, and it bothered me. She didn't carry it for bears. She wore it because she is a "resource manager" — and a cop.

"We don't want to be seen as cops," she said. "We want to be seen as rangers."

But the fact is that a park ranger's first job is to protect people against people. Their second priority is protecting people against the park, and last, the park against people.

Each night Yellowstone becomes a city of 16,000 people, and "anything that can happen in a city does and will happen in a national park," said Dan Sholly, Divine's boss and chief ranger.

Last year in Yellowstone a summer employee murdered another, one of 18 deaths in the park in 1985. Each was investigated as possibly suspicious.

This summer the park has had six rapes reported, a cocaine-dealer bust, 60 drunk-driving arrests, assaults on officers, demonstrations, several car thefts, someone with a blow torch cutting open campground fee boxes, and a passel of what cops call "domestics." If someone hears screaming and breaking glass in a room at Lake Hotel, a ranger knocks on the door.

Because Yellowstone was created before Wyoming, rangers enforce federal law and haul offenders before the park's own judge. Law enforcement here dates to 1876, when the Army was brought in to control poaching, logging and fires.

The new National Park Service, created in 1917, continued the tradition right down to the military-like uniform. Rangers take poaching training and patrol 350 miles of road, 1,000 miles of trail and 400 miles of unroaded boundary.

The shift I spent with Divine, she wrote a $50 ticket for fishing out of season to an employee who knew better, talked about bears with visitors, followed up on a thermal burn investigation and warned a group of tourists who were flashing strobes in a moose's face.

Later, in endless repetition, she warned campers that coolers needed to be locked inside at night because of bears.

"I usually think of a natural-resource reason for enforcing the law," she said.

In my summer here, I have seen a couple of instances when rangers simply confronted a visitor with the greeting: "That's against the law," without explaining why.

Rangers are somewhat possessive of the park — most are trained in natural sciences — and strapping on a gun can create a cop mentality.

Commissioned rangers must take 400 hours of law enforcement training and 40 hours of annual review. This year, for some, it included practice handling demonstrators — verbal judo, handcuff use and tear gas — because Earth First!, an environmental group, had threatened to close the park.

Divine, a ranger since 1978, said she fights the temptation to be possessive about the park. "I am protective," she said. Law enforcement at Yellowstone is as much explaining the park and its natural cycles as it is being an enforcer of federal laws, she said. "That's why I don't feel too much like a cop."

AUGUST 17

- - -

It's an odd feeling, standing on a huge rockslide, some of it paved over with roads and a parking lot, to know that 200 or 300 feet below lie 19 people.

Buried 27 years ago today, they were typical tourists, campers who probably had found Yellowstone full and had opted to camp along the Madison River, to the west. That night, a mountain fell on them, making them victims of forces that underlie this park.

Their deaths stirred a new interest in Yellowstone's geology that continues today.

According to one account, a geologist camped near Hebgen Lake the night of the 1959 earthquake ran out of his shaking trailer shouting, "It's mine. It's mine." Many more geologists swarmed into the park afterward.

Wayne Hamilton, who studies Yellowstone's volcanic activity today, is a bit more subdued. "It would be a mistake to think we understand this stuff," he said.

But since that earthquake, Yellowstone is considered less an oddity and more a living laboratory for the understanding and predicting of earthquakes and volcanoes.

The quake was the largest in the Rocky Mountains in recent history, about 7.1 on the Richter scale, and the 10th-largest in the United States. It created a new lake, tilted the land beneath Hebgen Lake, and left scars visible today. Witnesses say the land rolled like a flag in the wind.

Hamilton, a Yellowstone naturalist at the time, said the quake turned hot pools into geysers, turned springs dirty, and rolled the pavement, and lifted cars half a foot at Canyon Village. More important, he said, the quake led to the first full-scale geologic mapping of the park.

As a result, we now know that Yellowstone's geysers and steaming pools are the remnants of a huge volcano, a caldera 65 by 40 kilometers that spread ash to the Gulf of Mexico 600,000 years ago.

The volcano is related to a "hot spot," a fountain of molten mantle in the earth over which North America is sliding as it moves west. The hot spot burns its way northeastward at about an inch a year, which means that someday Yellowstone National Park may be in Duluth.

As it moves through the crust, much like a boat, it leaves earthquakes, volcanoes and the Snake River Valley in its wake. The 1959 earthquake was in that path. Last year in the area, 10,000 quakes, most of them minor, were recorded.

At the center of Yellowstone, the land is rising, like a balloon slowly inflating. Near Mud Volcano, the land is rising about an inch a year. Between 1923 and 1976, it rose three meters. The rise is caused by rock expanding as it is heated. When the volcano was discovered, many wondered if it was building to blow again. It is, said Hamilton, but not anytime soon.

In the meantime, the rising land at the outlet of Yellowstone Lake is deepening the lake, just like adding to a dam. And that's where Hamilton's work begins.

Plying the cold waters with a cranky park boat, this graying, slow-talking sailing nut has taken hundreds of sonar readings of submerged terraces, old beaches, that show the lake is rising.

Terraces above the lake, however, indicate that the lake level has gone up and down for the past 9,000 years. Hamilton's theory is that as the hot rock forming the new volcano expands and rises, it cracks and slumps.

"Yellowstone is very dynamic," he said. A volcanic eruption is not imminent, he said, but there will be severe earthquakes in the coming decades.

Still, to a layman like me, it is fascinating to think of this land on which I drive and fish ballooning upward beneath my feet. And fun to image the volcanoes blowing again, at the peak of the tourist season.

I can see Wayne Hamilton, riding the plume now, like Slim Pickens riding the bomb in "Dr. Strangelove" -- a geologist on the spot, yelling, "It's mine. It's mine."

AUGUST 19

- - -

They sat in the grass beside the Gibbon River, their faces many colors, and listened to how this park came to be more than a century ago. They had traveled from many nations, China, Zimbabwe, Samoa, Israel, on a pilgrimage of sorts.

"To come here," said one from Panama, "is to come to La Mecca."

Yellowstone, said another, was the "mother park."

"It was here," said a Swede. "It started everything."

On this spot in 1870, near where the Gibbon meets the Firehole River to form the Madison, the words "national park" were spoken by men around a campfire. Two years later, Congress created the park to protect the geysers.

The idea was not new. Europeans had hunting preserves. Switzerland established an animal preserve in the 15th century. China and Korea had parks hundreds of years ago.

Even in this country, at the height of the Industrial Revolution, saving wild lands for man's renewal was emerging as reason enough. And so, a national park, as we understand it today, was born with Yellowstone. It became the model for parks worldwide.

On their tour of Yellowstone this summer, park managers from foreign countries came to study again, to learn from our mistakes.

"We grab on to that with avarice," said Derek Potter, who runs nine South African parks. "It's like walking down a road at night behind a guy. Where he trips, you watch. We look at Yellowstone as an example of a system pushed to its limits by people. They seem to have found the balance."

In talking to these men and women, I found Yellowstone's problems pale by comparison. In Brazil, for example, forests that once covered 82 percent of Sao Paulo state have been reduced to four percent.

"I see here a well-planned park," said Fausto Pires de Campos. "You see the people having respect for the animal. In my country, every week I go and see people taking palm trees. You can see new roads into the mountains."

In rough English I did not quite understand, he told me of dealing with dictators and gold miners, timber companies and farmers, Indians and developers, all taking a piece of the public lands, despite laws.

Park visitors at Amboseli, in Kenya, leave the roads and drive around the African herds at will, said James Ochoki, deputy director for Kenya's wildlife. In Yellowstone, he said, vehicles at least are confined to the roads, leaving the rest of the park untouched.

Ochoki, educated at Howard University, said Kenya's attempts to control elephants by shooting have been controversial — not unlike Yellowstone's elk story. Yet there are not 20,000 elephants, confined unnaturally in one park. They are changing the ecology, he said, from a canopy forest to grasslands.

In Tanzania, the parks seem to be in good condition because they are "almost sacred," said Bakari Mbano, who runs a wildlife college. But they are rarely visited.

"The average citizen can't enjoy the parks because you need to drive into them," he said. "You must pay to get in. The facilities in the park are expensive and beyond the means of our people."

So who comes? I asked.

"Foreigners, like you."

AUGUST 21

- - -

Alston Chase was picking raspberries when I pulled up. His jeans had a big tear in the right knee surrounded by fresh red stains, his shirt was dirty, and big drops of sweat had surfaced far up his forehead into the few white hairs.

He walked through a thick crop of thistles that had gotten out of hand while he was away promoting his book, and offered me a berry.

His house, simple, open, filled with art and books and New York magazines, is high on a slope near the north edge of Paradise Valley. Fifty miles to the south is the subject of his book, "Playing God in Yellowstone — the Destruction of America's First National Park."

Since its release in May, Chase has been persona non grata in Yellowstone. Just the mention of his name sets park managers stuttering expletives. If I have heard one thing consistently from park people, it is that Chase is a liar.

For a man who already wears an expression bordering on wounded, such a description must cut deeply.

He is an academic, a graduate of Harvard, Oxford and Princeton, who adopted Montana gradually bringing his wife and three sons to vacation, then to buy a remote ranch, then to quit his philosophy teaching job at Macalester College to run environmental classes.

He began a book on the green revolution and its effect on Yellowstone. But he found inconsistencies between raw data and what the park was telling the public. The number of bears, for example, was inflated.

He said the park stonewalled him, forcing him to file Freedom of Information requests for information. He developed a "Deep

Throat" informant. Ultimately, he concluded the park was covering up.

Over a beer, I told him that in my summer here I had not found the same things he had. Park managers were open and honest, and there was a healthy internal debate about park policies. I also did not think the park service was destroying Yellowstone.

He smiled and said he would take part of the credit.

This year, the park service has stepped up research on areas of concern in the book, notably the size of the elk herd and the danger that it is eating other species out of house and home.

At the heart of Chase's book is "natural regulation." By pretending that Yellowstone is a natural area and keeping hands off — by not playing God, he argued — the park is killing the animals. Chase argues for more God playing.

Yet there are numerous instances in the park where man's hand is laid heavily, and maybe to good result. Chase makes no mention of them.

Fishing is one. Building floating nests for trumpeter swans is another. The park service uses herbicides on exotic weeds, it poisons streams to kill unwanted fish, it wants to reintroduced the wolf, which has all but been eliminated. And rangers fly bears around in helicopters as if they were pieces in a giant board game, trying to keep some semblance of a "natural" park.

I found Chase thoughtful and caring, a romantic who adopted the West yet remains aloof. He is the kind of person who almost got physically sick when a neighbor killed a mountain lion, and his Montana license plate reads, "Gadfly."

The book has isolated him further, I gather, cutting off even environmental groups, whom he slays as sleeping watchdogs.

I got the feeling that he is at home, isolated, surrounded by research papers, watching the Big Sky country from the windows of his study.

AUGUST 24

- - -

They say in Yellowstone country there are two seasons — winter and relatives.

When news got out that I had a foldout sofa on the porch, it was like issuing an invitation to the royal wedding. No one wanted to miss it, and a couple of people even tried to crash.

Doug and Pam, old friends from South Dakota, arrived last week; they had been invited. I had stocked up on food, bought a couple of bottles of the best Idaho wine I could get, and unfolded the sofa. For lack of space, privacy was abandoned.

We stayed up late talking and playing music, then they went to bed on the porch, closing the big board shutters against the cool night air. I'd get some work done then, sitting in one of the rockers with the computer in my lap, writing another letter.

During the day they wanted to see the park, and I wanted to show it to them. I'd squeeze in interviews between sights.

I took them to Old Faithful, to the Inn, then out along the geyser basin. We caught Daisy, Riverside and two Old Faithful eruptions. While they ate ice cream, I called the office.

At Fishing Bridge, we joined a nature walk to find the Troll, a strange-looking, masked creature that supposedly lives under the bridge and eats people who keep fish longer than 13 inches. To keep visitors safe, the ranger carried a "troll control," which looked to me like a squirt gun.

When we found him, the Troll explained through his rubber mask the importance of large fish, and Fishing Bridge, and picking up trash. Kids love him.

The program is a new one, part of an attempt by the naturalist staff to breathe life into Yellowstone's dumpy interpretation programs and displays.

The man who plays the Troll, for example, helped invent a Yellowstone game -- biologically correct right down to the predator-food chain. A video version is in the works. Toys for tots may be next, a mobile food chain, or a jigsaw ecosystem.

George Robinson is in charge of the interpretation program. I liked him immediately because his office walls are book-lined, and spare corners are plastered with cartoons and quotes from Dr Seuss. He believes, with Seuss, that there is a child in all of us, and the best programs appeal to that child.

He speaks eloquently of the need for wilderness and for slowing people down enough to catch a glimpse of it. Three hundred new roadside displays — that can't be read from a car — will help. So will innovative nature walks, like the Troll hunt.

For me, such walks at Yellowstone became the springboard for more personal exploration of the back country. They introduced me to plants and animal behavior and took the edge off apprehension we all feel in wild country.

As a result, I felt comfortable leading friends into places where we could tap the richest vein of this park.

Doug, Pam, my daughter Amy, and I hiked two miles to Cascade Lake, not much bigger than a pond, near Canyon Village. As the noise of traffic slipped away, we stopped to look at flowers, eat wild strawberries and grouse whortleberries — something I never knew existed before a naturalist enlightened me.

We had lunch by the lake, alone except for a gull and an occasional fish splashing to the surface. And then we lay down in the tall sharp grass and napped in the sun.

"Yellowstone is a place where we can re-establish our ties with the real world," Robinson told me. "To sense, sometimes for the first time, the primeval, elemental interrelationship between humans and their planet. To be alone, just for a few minutes with the wellspring of our lives and the things we need to survive — clean air, clean water, open space. I believe there is a spark in all of us, of connectedness."

Later that day, we joined the crowds for a glimpse of the Grand Canyon, and the lower falls. It was spectacular. But Doug and Pam said later that the walk to the lake had been the highlight of their trip.

AUGUST 25

- - -

As the helicopter lifted off, blowing the slough grasses and
shattering the wilderness calm, we did not know how badly Bill was
injured.

But we felt better, knowing that he was hospital-bound, off the
ground where he had lain in agony by the campfire all night.

There was something terribly wrong with his left leg. It was
lifeless, numb and cold. When we carried him up from the creek, it
had dragged behind, his foot limp. Into the night we felt ignorant and
isolated, listening to him groan. And so at 1:30 a.m. I set off for the
trailhead, eight miles away, for help.

In the backcountry of Yellowstone, we come face to face with
our strengths — and inadequacies, which I was feeling then. Here,
common sense scuffles with risk taking.

I did not like walking alone in moonlit fog through bear
country. I knew bears were there. I had been briefed by a ranger
before setting off with Bill and Jerry and my daughter, Amy. We had
judged it an acceptable risk and had thought it the only one.

Bill Jordan and Jerry Lewis are Colorado newspapermen who
have backpacked and fished together for years. After the hot hike,
we set up camp. We raised the food on ropes. The tents went up
along Slough Creek, gorgeous water so clear we could watch the
trout rise.

Bill was captivated. He waded in barefoot and fished a riffle
for two or three hours while the rest of us staked out pools
downstream. Behind him the Absaroka Ridge turned pink toward
evening.

That's when I heard Amy yell for help. Bill had slipped against
a rock and fallen into the water. When I got there, he was lying on
the gravel, crying in pain. His left leg had cramped, he thought.

He was in shock and cold. Jerry and I stripped him, put him in the sleeping bag and started coffee. I lay with him in the mummy bag the best I could, trying to warm him.

Bill cried out when he moved. But we had to get him to a fire. There, we placed bottles of hot water along his leg. He began to sweat, but the pain did not stop and his leg was still cold. He could not feel me pinch below his groin, and he could not move his toes.

That's when I went for help. At 3:30 a.m., I awoke a trail crew and asked them to radio for a ranger.

Every summer in Yellowstone, backcountry rangers deal with injuries that would challenge emergency room doctors. They use horses, boats, helicopters and their own legs to find and rescue. So far this year, there have been 33 missions, and helicopters have been called 20 times.

This time, special permission was given to drive the trail to the campsite, but the three rangers were delayed by a gate locked at the trailhead. They began to saw through it at one end and jack it out of the ground at the other. Before they finished, the lock's combination was radioed from a private ranch. Then they bent a rim on a rock, and had to stop to change the tire.

It was light when we walked into camp. Ranger Tom Goldsmith, a doctor, decided to call in a medical helicopter from Billings. He suspected a fracture, but Bill also had a heart murmur, which worried him.

By 9 a.m. the chopper was on the ground. As they loaded Bill, we kidded him about the drama of it all and took his picture. By 10 it was raining hard and we were bumping our way back to the trailhead.

By the time I got back to my cabin, Bill was heading to surgery at a Billings hospital. He was lucky to be alive.

In a six-hour operation, doctors found an aneurysm in his aorta and inserted a Dacron replacement. For some reason, the aneurysm had blocked circulation in his leg. There was danger he could lose his leg because it had been without blood for 18 hours.

Three days after the surgery, he still had no feeling in, nor use of, his leg, but doctors were optimistic they could save it.

What more could have been done? Jerry and I lashed ourselves with that question.

Not going would have been the safest, but in that security we would have gained nothing. In wilderness risk there is a challenge that awakens and enriches us. I think that even Bill, roused from his hospital bed, would have agreed.

(Bill Jordan kept his leg and was able to walk again. He passed away in 2002.)

AUGUST 29

- - -

Mosquito Creek runs through a pretty valley south of Wilson, Wyo., little known and little used despite a fairly good dirt road that climbs with the stream away from the Snake River wet to the Snake River Ranger.

The day I drove it, I saw one tent in a meadow and two people on horseback. The road had been washed by a thunderstorm, and the flowers and trees stood out sharp and fresh in the sun.

So pristine is this place that Congress has designated it a wilderness study area. I tried to imagine an industrial complex here: pipelines, gas wells, power lines and traffic. I couldn't.

The Anschutz Corp. can, however. Its application to drill a test well for gas along Mosquito Creek is creating a stir in Jackson. Opponents say the well is another threat to the Yellowstone area. There is so much untouched land in the Yellowstone area, I questioned whether it was truly threatened.

An ecologist from the Wilderness Society answered this way: imagine Yellowstone as a giant tapestry, rich and colorful — a mosaic of scenic beauty, wildlife and wildness. For every animal killed, he said, remove a thread. For every gas well, remove another thread. For every development or timber road, another thread or two.

The tapestry will remain, he said, but over time become threadbare. I tucked that image into my head as I drove counterclockwise around the park.

On the north side, I talked with gentleman rancher Len Sargent, who owns a corner of paradise bordering the park and the Gallatin National Forest. He is fighting a Forest Service proposal for road access across this property to the public woodlands. Hunters from Billings want to hunt elk there. The feds want to get at their land. But Forest Service roads are notorious routes for poachers.

Several of Sargent's neighbors have drilled small geothermal wells for heat, drilling allowed by Montana. But they may be tapping the same system that plumbs the Mammoth Hot springs.

A proposal to develop a major geothermal field in Idaho, adjacent to the park, was tabled for fear of what it might do to the park's geysers. That's a threat I can picture clearly.

Near West Yellowstone, a man is proposing a ski area in bear country. The town, struggling for year-round survival, would like to see it. But bears who roam there would have to move, or die.

West of there, on the Henry's Fork River, world famous for its trout and fly fishing, developers have proposed six hydroelectric dams. I can't imagine a river with such a tradition being damned, but to prevent the dams, someone in Washington may have to outlaw them. According to the Sierra Club, oil and gas leases have been issued on half of the public land around the park, including sites at four of Yellowstone's five entrances. Several gas wells are proposed within sight of the Grand Tetons.

Most of the 160 wells drilled in the Bridger-Teton National Forest have been dry, but there is geologic promise, and oil companies are not giving up.

At the Triangle X Dude Ranch north of Jackson, John Turner, one of three brothers who runs it, jerked a thumb toward the back of his ranch, to logging clear-cuts and roads that riddle the area.

Hunters now have easy access to what once was a trophy herd heading south to the Jackson Hole Elk Refuge. Turner, a biologist, says that hunting has reduced the size of the herd and forced it to change migration routes.

On the east side of the park, there is logging and gas leasing. Back on the north side, near Gardiner, a gold mine may crank up again, raising concerns about pollution from chemical processes.

There is a saying I hear often from people who love the parks and forests: "Once it's gone, it's gone."

They don't mean the whole tapestry, I now realize. Their concern is with each thread, being pulled one at a time.

There will always be a Yellowstone. The question is, how rich and beautiful — how valuable — will it be?

AUGUST 31

- - -

In the mind of a child, what remains after a trip through
Yellowstone?

Bears and fish, buffalo and geysers? An environmental ethic?
Or just memories of good times with Dad.

Along the Madison River yesterday, I stopped at every kid I
could find. There weren't many, because school has started. Without
them Yellowstone is a different park.

Why, I asked people along the river, do you bring your
children here? Do they appreciate it?

"I honestly don't think so," said a father from New Jersey.
"But it's sowing a seed for future appreciation of nature."

His boys, 6 and 7 years old, were playing at the water's edge.
One came running to the van for a bucket "to catch fish."

In the same picnic spot, several mothers were sitting on
blankets in the shade, their children scattered. They had seen a
moose that morning outside their tent.

"They do understand that this is one place where you can see
all these things," a mother from Washington said. So much can be
seen from the road; yet at a picnic area they can run free.
As her boy, Jasper, ran by, she grabbed him and asked, "What do you
like most?"

"Having licorice," he smacked.

Down the road, George Bradley was parking a camper with his
son Doug, the start of a few days together in the park. They had
visited a decade ago, but Doug, 23, was grown now, his father
graying. And they are apart most of the year, in Cincinnati and Fort
Collins. I asked them whether coming here brought them closer.

"Oh sure," said George. "It can't hurt," said Doug.

102

Bringing children to Yellowstone I think, fulfills two adults needs. We get to see these wonders ourselves, with our families. But more important, we get to pass on something, a bit of our heritage.

I hope my own daughter left with a whole forest sown in her heart, a little bit of me, and a lot of what this park can teach on its own.

Hiking together and camping in the back country, which we did, could become a lifelong habit. And how do you measure the importance to her, and this park, of seeing a moose cow and calf in the wild one day and two black bears eating garbage the next?

Here in the cabin, she picked up a book and read of Yellowstone's early days, of Teddy Roosevelt's visit and the words of John Burroughs. She asked about Burroughs, the pioneer conservationist.

She also began to complain, quite vocally, about tourists who stop suddenly in the middle of the road to watch buffalo. She had been with me long enough.

Amy's one request, spoken at the beginning of the summer, was to catch a fish and cook it for supper.

The last day before her school began, we hired a guide on Yellowstone Lake, trolled deep below the algae bloom, and found a couple of cutthroat small enough to keep. Her smile was unforgettable.

So was our supper, with bread she had baked, and fish she had caught, and memories of a summer in Yellowstone.

SEPTEMBER - DECEMBER

SEPTEMBER 1

- - -

The slide into autumn in Yellowstone has been subtle this year. No snowstorm. No hard freeze. It was still hot enough yesterday to hike with my shirt off.

In the morning, though, Joe Zarki scraped frost off his windshield at Canyon Village. He also heard the first bugles from anxious elk, a certain sound of fall.

The meadows are turning golden now, the grasses dying. A patch of aspen seedlings on Dunraven Pass had turned, too — I thought prematurely.

As usual, Mother Nature is well along in her preparation for winter. It just took someone with Zarki's naturalist eye to find the evidence.

The asters are about the only flowers left, those and a few yellow cinquefoil that remind me of buttercups. The rest have gone to seed, the cow parsnip, the lupine that last month blanketed this park. Sticky geranium leaves are turning bright red in the undergrowth. And the tiny yellow flowers of sage are in bloom.

The butterflies we saw were drab and flea-bitten, except for the angel wings, hatching now and providing some of the last flashes of color in the dying meadow. In Hayden Valley, the buffalo are herding up earlier than usual, the bulls rejoining the mothers and calves.

If I had asked Zarki two months ago about autumn, he would have pointed to the sandpipers, heading south. There have been large numbers of American avocets, marbled godwits and long-billed curlews, stopping during their migrations.

"They are the first signs that summer is on the wane," he said.

Zarki has somewhat of the mad-scientist look about him, with blond hair hanging long on each side of a bald spot, glasses, and a moustache that looks as if it was pasted on askew. He is a birder, and by watching them he sees early signs of the season's change.

Down on the Yellowstone River, ducks are molting, using the water to protect themselves during the time they can't fly.

The red-tailed hawks are soaring often, hunting, building fat reserves for their migration to the Gulf Coast.

In the pines, Clark's Nutcrackers are gathering and burying pine nuts. This has not been a good year for pine nuts, which are a traditional source of fat for grizzly bears.

As a result, the bears have come down from higher elevations and gone into campgrounds and villages. After walking with Zarki, I watched a grizzly and two cubs just up Dunraven road. She was digging yampa roots. A few days earlier she had been in Canyon Village, looking for human food.

Bears have been in the West Yellowstone, too, one right behind my cabin, foraging in a dumpster, and another broke into a house on the other side of town.

Only in isolated nooks can you see snow patches still in the park, like high on the northeast of Mount Washburn. Yet it won't be long before the bears climb up there and dig beneath new snow, to hibernate until spring.

SEPTEMBER 5

- - -

I took one last ride through the park yesterday — sitting in a stuffed chair in a living room, sipping a Diet Pepsi, seeing Yellowstone through the eyes of an RV family.

They were a modest household, grandparents from Oregon taking their grandkids on a tour of America. Yellowstone was the first stop.

Their RV was modest, too, compared with many I've seen this summer. Twenty-seven feet long, 7-1/2 feet wide, two TVs, a microwave, a couch that folded into a bed, a bathroom, a 110-generator started with a button on the dash, and a tape deck.

As we headed for Old Faithful, the two kids punched in the Beach Boys, watched through the big picture window windshield and sang along. Andy Stare, the 71-year-old grandpa, drove and talked.

"We want to make the Grand Canyon, the Petrified Forest, Meteor Crater, Carlsbad Cavern, Mount Rushmore, Niagara Falls, West Point, the Statue of Liberty, Revolutionary and Civil War battlefields, Washington, D.C. Dawn wants to go to Maine. Darrel wants Florida. We're going down the Blue Ridge Parkway, 470 miles, from one end to the other."

The itinerary was on three sheets of lined paper, a day for each line, 85 days in all. They had until 4 p.m. to see Yellowstone.

They knew there were animals in the park and geysers, but little else. Andy wheeled into a likely looking parking area along the Firehole River, and they walked the boardwalks. They touched the hot water, they walked in steam, they took pictures with a small camera.

"Get a ladle of that," Andy joked at a bubbling paint pot. "We'll have that for lunch."

Andy, crew-cut and solid, was a retired Army mechanic who had been overseas. His wife, Mina, was from Kentucky. She had a pretty smile and a permanent. They always had dreamed of an RV — sleeping on the ground did not appeal to Mina — but they never thought they could afford one.

Finally, they moved from their home near Los Angeles to the woods of Oregon, leaving behind noise and crime and a multi-racial neighborhood. On the bumper was the sticker, "We're spending our kid's inheritance."

Darren, 13, and Dawn, 16, are taught at home by their mother, from a Christian correspondence school. Andy said they were old enough now to appreciate America.

"This is the only place you'll ever see this," Andy lectured as they walked past Clepsydra, a geyser. "Smells like rotten eggs doesn't it?"

Mina pointed to dead stumps nearby. "Wonder how long it takes those trees to petrify. We'll have to get a book at a gift shop."

They arrived at Old Faithful five minutes before it erupted. They stood on the boardwalk behind the benches. When it erupted, Mina took Andy's arm.

"Well, I'm glad we lived this long to make this trip," she told him.

Back at the RV, she started the generator and made tuna melt in an electric skillet. Andy said grace and we sat around a table that fit into holes in the floor.

"Why did you come to Yellowstone?" I asked them.

"We had never seen it," said Andy. "It's part of our heritage, our country, and we need to see it."

Mina offered me a cookie as Andy continued.

"Every young man should go overseas," he said. "They need to see what other people have to contend with, and compare it with what we have here."

He wanted to drive the big loop of Yellowstone, but I told him he didn't have time. I suggested he take in the Yellowstone falls and drive through Hayden Valley before heading to Cody.

The windows and loose pots rattled as we drove. Mina sat on the couch and watched through the lace curtains.

"Wonder if there are many fish up here?" she said. "I wonder where all that water comes from?"

In diaries the kids listed the animals they'd seen: moose, trumpeter swans, geese, a squirrel, a couple of elk, ducks, a crow, a fox, and a small buffalo herd.

Just beyond the herd, the RV ran out of gas and coasted to a stop. The RV got six miles per gallon. Andy switched to a second tank.

At the mud volcano they stopped to crunch through the hail that covered the road, but they were not interested in seeing any more geysers. It was nearly 3:30. They stopped at Fishing Bridge to let me off.

"Your parents should come here," Mina said to the children.

"Yeah," said Dawn. "If Dad could get away."

"And spend a week and see it," added Andy. "We need to come back and spend a week here, and take some trails. Get off the beaten path. But in order to take it all in, we need to keep moving."

Mina looked out the steamed-over window. "I hope they got some rain at home."

SEPTEMBER 7

- - -

The air in Yellowstone had a certain snap to it this morning. I scraped frost off the car and backed it to the door of the cabin to begin packing for the trip home.

It was the same air I felt three months ago when I drove in, through snow, in search of some meaning in this park.

I slept uneasily then, in anticipation. I woke before dawn again today, fearing I had missed something.

Yesterday, while I was showing a friend the geyser basin a fella from Fargo walked by, stopped to take a video of Beauty Pool, and remarked, "A guy could spend a whole day here." I nearly laughed out loud. A guy could spend three months here, as I did, and not see it all.

This was even more apparent to me the day I hiked to the fire tower on Mount Washburn to reflect. I could see 25 miles in each direction, not nearly the whole park. Rain was falling to the west. Birds were riding the wind around me. Not far below, big horn sheep were greeting hikers on the trail.

I was surprised at how mountainous the park was. Down in the Yellowstone canyon was a trail I had missed. Off to the southwest was Shoshone Lake, which I didn't see this summer. And way off to the south was an area as wild and untouched as any place in the world, and I had missed that, too.

What, pray tell, had the 2 million visitors this summer missed? Driving through in a few hours? Or a mere week?

I guess they got out of this park what they invested in it.

For me, Yellowstone was an extraordinary experience. I climbed a mountain, helped save a man's life, pondered the meaning of wilderness without the grizzly, and saw water and rocks and flowers and birds in a new way. I grew as a writer.

110

I began, too, to feel like a caretaker, however puny and transitory, in this park's passage through time. More than once I stopped fishermen along the Yellowstone River in Hayden Valley to tell them they were fishing in the wrong spot.

I was nagged by the issues here, still unresolved, as to whether this park should be tampering with, or preserving, nature.

I worried, too, about the "value" of this park to Americans — if, say, they had to choose between an oil well and the habitat for a couple of grizzlies. My fear was that the man driving an RV, giving six miles per gallon-was already casting his vote.

Many people kidded me about my "paid vacation" in Yellowstone. But I was so totally immersed in it I could not enter the park just for fun. Each time I did, another letter occurred to me or I'd strike up a conversation and scribble a quote. Back at the cabin, I put myself to sleep with Yellowstone history. I ate breakfast on a table strewn with bear mortality charts.

So it's time, after 39 letters, for a break. I may be the only man in the world who needs to get out of Yellowstone, to "get away."

P.S. This isn't the end of Letters from Yellowstone. I'll return in December to ski and snowmobile and watch Old Faithful frost the air every hour or so. They tell me it's a different world in winter.

DECEMBER 14

- - -

When I returned, West Yellowstone had the look of a town hunched against the cold. The ragtag building shapes, softened by a foot of snow, seemed to lean together for warmth.

Wood, stockpiled all summer and fall, now fed the cold air. It was 6 degrees at high noon when I drove in. At sunup it was 22 below.

The cabin seemed squat in the snow, ringed by icicles that hung from the eaves. The porch, where I had written in the summer sun, was now stuffed with wood, the doorway framed with evergreen boughs.

Inside, a fire was going. My landlords, Tom and Dorit Herman, had decorated a young fir with Christmas lights and spread boughs on tables and cabinets. Tom turned on the lights and I unpacked.

The requirement was simple this time — keep warm. I brought every heavy shirt, every piece of wool and my felt-lined boots. I would live in them, I suspected.

I brought, too, Christmas cards and gifts, for I would be here until the New Year, continuing to write, as I had during the summer, about Yellowstone and what national parks mean to us.

For some weeks now, the park has been closed to vehicles with tires. It opened this weekend to snowmobiles.

I drove to West Yellowstone, just outside the park. The closer I got, the more I felt I had entered a white spacescape, wiped clean of people. Winter had transformed this land I had become familiar with.

Gone was West Yellowstone's t-shirt row, boarded over. Gone were the grizzlies, to hibernation. Gone were the RVs. Gone were the fly fishermen.

Fred Terwilliger, who owns Bud Lilly's fly shop, was alone when I walked in, watching the four-wheel-drives pass by his big windows.

"We're not bothered by too many customers," he said smiling. "Once in a while we sell a pair of wool socks." Even if fishing were allowed, he said, ice in the guides on the pole would make it a nuisance.

Winter transforms West Yellowstone into a man's town, several women told me, with rugged outdoor activity: snowmobiling, splitting wood, thawing pipes. No movie, no music, no place to go, said silversmith Nancy Hull.

Even men admit to psychological problems with so much isolation and cold.

"I don't like it," said Bob Leithead, who earns part of his living thawing pipes. "I don't sleep good. I worry about the cars not starting and what's happening to the house."

I caught him heading out the door to fix a broken pipe 6 feet beneath a trailer. Already it was 10 to 15 below and the air was white with cold, like looking through a frosted window. Leithead called it Yellowstone frost.

But inside, my log cabin was toasty. I slipped some vegetables to stew on the wood stove, and Tom showed me how to stoke the fire and damp it down to keep it burning while I slept beneath a pile of quilts.

If it got really cold, like the 50 or 60 below that West Yellowstone is famous for, Tom suggested I take special precautions.

He pointed to a jug next to some bubblebath by the tub. It was antifreeze. After my bath, he said, pour a little into the drain to keep the trap from freezing.

DECEMBER 17

- - -

Pity the poor buffalo. All he wanted was to roam. What he got was center stage in a slapstick farce, surrounded by sober faces. I may be the only one who thinks it's funny.

Here was this great lumbering symbol of America, trying to leave Yellowstone. Being harassed by hunters, lawyers, cattlemen and rangers.

"Get back," they shouted, "or die!"

Buffalo have wandered away from the park for generations. But a decade ago, at the northern entrance, a few found they could walk to greener pastures down plowed roads. No more cold feet in the Lamar Valley snow. The word spread. Each year a few more came. Last year there was 300 at, or across, the park boundary.

During most of that same decade, Montana game wardens shot the animals as they crossed the line — with the park's blessing. Montana didn't want the brucellosis that half of them carry.

But the kill got out of hand. Three years ago it was 40. Two years ago 88. The Montana Legislature approved a buffalo hunt — if you could call it that.

Last year, when buffalo left the park, hunters were chosen by lottery, called, escorted to the docile giants, and told to shoot. There were more cameras than guns. In West Yellowstone, one was shot in a graveyard and fell on a headstone, knocking it over.

Then the Fund for Animals got involved, suing the park for failing to preserve its wildlife. The fund is famous for painting baby seals and herding wild burros. Saving an American symbol had certain sex appeal.

At first the park resisted, hiding behind its philosophy that the buffalo should be able to roam. Neighbors argued that such a policy essentially allowed the buffalo to expand park boundaries.

This fall, bowing to pressure, rangers built a fence, installed a cattle guard, and tried, in various ways, to shoo the buffalo away from their newfound trail.

A couple of bulls scrambled around the edge of the cattle guard. One went straight across — 15 feet. His feet were big enough to span the gaps.

Ah, buffalogate.

Rangers went on special 24-hour patrol, sounding sirens, playing wolf calls, firing plastic bullets and firecrackers. They build a second fence and made aerial reconnaissance.

Last week, when Montana found 30 buffalo outside the park it called a hunt. The morning the hunters arrived, the buffalo had skipped back across the border.

When I left the north gate a couple of days ago, about 100 buffalo were grazing contentedly where they weren't supposed to be.

The Fund for Animals, which had a lawyer on the scene, thinks the ultimate solution is buffalo birth control. Its lawsuit was grinding along with enough depositions to make another barrier.

Back in the park, the other 2,000 buffalo were just trying to survive another winter. No one knew what they thought of all this.

But many people were raising their assessment of buffalo intelligence. Left to their own devices, someone said, they would repopulate the Great Plains.

I did see this: some smart alecs among them had left frozen comment on the road. Right on the edge, of the wrong side, of the buffalogate.

DECEMBER 19

- - -

For a while, after I shut down the snow machine and my ears emptied of the road, I pretended I had Yellowstone to myself.

I was standing behind Old Faithful, in a parking lot by the inn and the visitor center. The snow had drifted randomly about the buildings, through the portico where smelly buses idled in summer, atop the half-moon of benches, along the wooden boardwalk through the geyser basin.

I walked slowly, creeping almost. It was spooky even in mid-afternoon. Inside the visitor center the desk stood empty, the clock running. There was no one to record the next eruption.

A half-mile away, Castle Geyser was blowing, and I walked the path to it with difficulty. The snow was crusty. Alongside, a brook ran, warm and enough to flow, but cool enough on the edges to allow scallops of ice and delicate flowers of frost to form.

Not far away, where the snow had melted, buffalo grazed on meager greens. Their path was marked with frozen chips. I gave one a good kick.

In the chill air, Castle spewed a white column like an old train at full steam, stuck in place. The steam twisted as it rose and spread, pure white against a winter blue sky.

Being here alone fascinated me. For about a month Yellowstone had been resting, its roads collecting snow, its ice cream shops cooling behind plywood covers.

In that time, the animals had moved to the lower regions, along the rivers, or out of the park, girding for winterkill that inevitably would take some of them.

The park has just reopened to people on sleds, skis and snow machines. But I was ahead of the crowd. As I drove a snowmobile in, elk lay in the snow next to the Madison River, or pawed through the cover to graze. An eagle flew the watercourse.

The trees cast stark shadows from a slant sun. Along the Firehole River, the trees were thickly flocked from the fog that rose from the water. More than once, a coyote crossed my path, unafraid, scavenging.

Coming to the flats at Hell's Half Acre, I stopped short at the view. White and white and blue. Steam from a wide, white plain, from pots and pools that bubbled as if there were no winter. This was heaven, not hell.

I could be the first, or the last, man here. It was not ego awash, or possessive ownership, even. In one sense, I wished to share it. But solitary, I was alone with my thoughts. I felt part of something. Infinity? Creation? How can I explain it? This was something I had to feel alone.

I shivered as Castle played out, and stepped to the walk's edge to leave a sign, a scent to mark my presence, the limits to my territory.

I turned to walk back to Old Faithful, to see it alone. How rare a privilege, even in winter.

Before I got there, she erupted, short and beautiful. Then I heard cheering. I topped the boardwalk to find 25 people in snowmobile suits. They seemed as surprised to see me. Maybe I had spoiled it for them, too.

There is in all of us a need to wonder, to discover, and Yellowstone has more than its share of such moments. Each time an animal shows, or a geyser erupts, or the sun shines in a particular way.

Each is new, and now, and gone. No wonder we try to lock those moments away in our hearts.

DECEMBER 21

- - -

The fun began with the snowcoach — a crazy cross between a school bus and something the Germans might have used to invade Russia in midwinter.

We got into it on a morning when the air cracked with ice crystals, and as it lumbered down the road we shouted to each other what we did and where we came from.

It wasn't long before someone cracked a flask of peach schnapps and passed it around. We took turns standing in the porthole, taking pictures of animals outside and joking about the wild life inside. We sprayed the windows with antifreeze. I passed out chocolate chip cookies. Alan, our driver, shouted back history and tidbits on what we were seeing.

By the time we got to Old Faithful, we were warm and friends and ready to ski. We skipped lunch and took off on a 3-mile track.

Grace and Carl were from Pittsburgh and were accomplished Nordic skiers. Renee, from Santa Cruz, was a beginner. Nancy, from Missoula, had skied a little.

There are only a couple hundred rooms at the Snowlodge — simple, quiet, rustic. Cut off from automobiles, Old Faithful in winter is close to sane. The huge parking lot becomes a snowfield, cut only by cross-country ski tracks. The only way in is by snowmobile or snowcoach.

After dinner, a couple of us strolled in the near full moonlight, down the geyser basin. I had seen magic here before, but this was new. The moon on the snow, the moon through the steam. We didn't talk much.

It was quiet in the lodge. The bartender fixed her special, a hot buttered rum, and she didn't stay open late. There are 75 miles of ski trail around Old Faithful, and skiers at this altitude crash early.

It was still below zero when we left for the Lone Star Geyser the next morning — four miles away. The sun was just yellowing the tops of trees, cutting through haze that had collected overnight.

We laughed at our hair turned white with frost. With a faceful I was the oldest.

We climbed sharply at first, through crystalline forests, the sun in our eyes. Every turn was a picture. I felt, at times, like taking off through untracked snow.

We crossed little streams and skied under lodgepoles bent halfway to the ground. We slipped right by a spike elk pawing through the snow.

After gaining 500 feet, we found the path a joy, running across a couple of high meadows, down a couple of hills. We whooped as we tried to stay erect down a path as slick and narrow as a luge run. They badly need snow.

Lone Star stood dramatically in a clearing, smoking and promising an eruption. We drank cider and shared an orange.

I left them there, new friends that I'll probably never see again. We didn't really get to know each other. We passed like skiers on a trail.

But the laughs were as good as any I've had. And we shared, for a while, a wonderland. It was just enough.

DECEMBER 23

- - -

The first sleigh ride of the season through the Jackson elk herd was like a visit to a great cathedral. People sat hushed on two long pews. Their tone, when they talked, was reverent.

"This is like the foliage of New England," said one old boy from Kansas. "The pictures don't do it justice."

Seven thousand elk were spread as far as we could see. Down from their mountain homes to a winter refuge. As the sled stopped near a six-point bull, we ran our cameras dry of film.

"I could look at them all day," said a hunter from Oregon.

The winter elk herd has become a major tourist attraction in Jackson Hole — 25,000 people took the sleigh ride last year. The Kansan and two farmer friends drove up just for that. "My wife said I was crazy," he said. "But aren't they beautiful."

Here, as nowhere else in Yellowstone country, one can sense what American wildlife must have been, the great herds that pioneers saw and slaughtered. Here, on this sleigh ride, I felt an innate love for these wild things.

Yet, here too, is an example of man's heavy-handed management of the wild. Our desire, or need, to fit it into our world.

The Jackson herd, which totals 25,000, is controlled by supplemental feeding on one hand, and hunting on the other. It is a balance kept for hunters and ranchers and a public that wants to see the great herds but does not want the elk to starve by the thousands.

There was a time in Yellowstone Park when elk died in droves in winter. Rangers, responding to the outcry, began controlling the elk population with roundups. But the roundups became slaughters themselves, and the cry was just as loud.

Today, the park service leaves management of its herd to nature. With a few mild winters, the park's northern herd has grown to 16,000.

There are many outside the park who feel that the herd has grown too large and that thousands could starve to death during a severe winter. Others feel the winter range, including aspen and willow growth, has been ruined by the huge herd. That, in turn, might be the reason streams have muddied, and other wildlife declined — the beaver, for one.

The park is studying those possibilities, but still thinks the herd has reached its natural level and that the herd won't ruin the park or die off in great numbers.

While there are always elk to see in the park, snow bunches them on their winter range — along rivers, in the Lamar Valley, at Mammoth Hot Springs. There, they eke out a living, even on the superintendent's lawn.

I drove through the Lamar Valley last week — the only road open to cars in winter — and gawked at the hundreds and hundreds of buffalo and elk.

There is something majestic about the way the way they move in winter, slowly, conserving energy, pawing and nosing their way to feed.

At sunset, near Pebble Creek, the moon came up full behind a herd. The setting sun had tinted the mountains pink. The snow was rose, the elk dark against it.

I took pictures until, again, I ran out of film. I know they won't do justice to what I saw.

DECEMBER 25

- - -

I must have looked like a space-age Santa, roaring through Yellowstone on a snowmobile. My pack was on my back, a helmet on my head; the shadow I cast was an astronaut on a rocket sled.

But the only gift I bore was a bottle of wine for a winter keeper. The rest was survival gear, sleeping bag and socks. I was headed to the interior of Yellowstone, and I went prepared.

It was snowing and cold, and wind found cracks in my armor. My moustache, wet from my breath, froze to the faceplate. My fingers cramped from jamming the throttle.

I was looking for a Christmas story and someone had told me about Steve Fuller.

Since 1972, Fuller has been winter keeper at the Grand Canyon of the Yellowstone. His job was to scrape off 250 inches of snow that falls on the roofs of 60 cabins and half-a-dozen other bigger buildings that are empty in the winter. This was his 14th winter in Yellowstone.

I found his driveway, a single snowmobile track, and pulled up to the house, modest, brown shingled, at home against the hill. I turned off the motor and sat and listened. I could still hear a roar.

Down below, in the midst of thick lodgepole, the two great falls of the Yellowstone River plunged. Mist rose above the trees, hundreds of feet, along with the sound.

"Come in," a voice yelled, vaguely British. I tramped in and peeled clothes in the warmth of the kitchen, dripping on the linoleum.

"You want something hot?" he said. "I've been hoping you'd ask for miles," I said. We shook hands. He was in his forties and had the build and grip of a high school wrestler. He fixed the first of many teas. I sat at the big pine table.

Steve found this job and the house that went with it after years of travel. Born in the Midwest, he met his British wife, Angela, in Britain and followed her to East Africa, where they taught school. She followed him, in turn, to the States.

"I wanted to develop a relationship with a place," he said. But to say he "settled down" would not be true. He devoured books. He chewed ideas. Working alone in the Yellowstone winters, his mind wandered.

As I listened, he stood in his kitchen in wool pants and suspenders and talked of Vietnam, China — his field of study — and Africa. We tussled with Yellowstone, with the destruction of nature.

"How can you be such an optimist?" he demanded.

"Because I seek out people with hope," I said.

"Do you read?" he said.

"Not enough."

I clung to my notebook in his sea of knowledge. Nuclear warheads, population overshoot, military incompetence, bureaucratic dynamics. His dam was bursting.

A piano played in the next room, the melody line to a carol. I stuck my head in and saw the tree and the girls, Emma, 14, and 12-year-old Skye. Their mother, Angela, was still at work at Mammoth, where she manages the park hotel. Steve crawled in the attic for the girls' ice skates, and we went outside.

Beneath the Otter Creek viaduct, the ice was thick and smooth. We played until we got cold, then went home for supper. Steve and the girls huddled at the stove and soon beef curry and fresh bread filled the pine table.

Fourteen years ago, the Fullers were alone in the heart of the park, before winter tourism had grown to support a small year-round community at Canyon. They shopped once in the fall, got mail every six weeks, and rarely saw a tourist.

The kids were taught at home, indoors and out. They read from books and learned stories told in tracks in the snow.

Steve also began taking photographs, for he saw a park few ever had. Of reeling beauty, of fire and ice, life and death.

"Yellowstone is a reminder of the real rules of the game," he said. "The Chinese call it living correctly — in harmony with heaven."

In time, Steve's photos began appearing, in Audubon, the National Geographic, on postcards and posters and prints. He became, in a graphic way, Yellowstone's winter keeper.

We talked until the moon rose. Steve threw open a window and looked out. By winter's end, he would have to shovel the windows clear on the lee side. I fell asleep by the tree, with moonlight on the tinsel.

At sunrise, while the girls slept, Steve and I went to the rim of the Canyon. From a thermal across the way, a river of mist flowed into the valley. Ravens drifted by. Rainbows formed in the water crystals. For two years he has watched this spot, waiting for the right moment to take a photograph.

We walked down to the lip of the upper falls. The water ran green. Mist sprayed and froze plaster on the canyon wall.

We drove our snow machines upriver to Yellowstone Lake, to hear, if we could, the music of ice forming. At Steamboat Point we walked past two buffaloes resting at a hot vent, and took pictures of ice formations along the lake's edge. Round holes in the ice bubbled with hot springs. They were warm to the touch. At noon we went home to hot lentil soup and rolls.

The Fuller house has always been a warm spot in the long nights of the Christmas season. Steve used to keep a light in the window, for the lost traveler.

"That was part of the tradition," he said. "I was humanity's representative."

Christmas guests were directed over Dunraven Pass, a 19-mile untracked ski to the house. "You feel like you've arrived somewhere after doing that."

Angela and the girls used to spend three days preparing — Yorkshire pudding, sausage rolls, pork pie. They baked and made candy and tree decorations of dough.

This year, with Angela running the hotel in Mammoth, the girls would carry on, until she got home Christmas Eve. Then they would leave cognac and cookies for Santa.

After lunch the four of us rode the snow machines through Hayden Valley, past herds of buffalo grazing in the snow, geese on open water. Haze lay like down on the soft curves of the landscape.

At Mud Volcano, Steve led us beyond the boardwalk — government trails, he called them — to uncharted hot pools. We walked on game trails, where the buffalo had broken the snow.

He put his arms around the girls. They talked gently, like friends of long standing.

Toward dark we stopped at a warm spot by a frozen lake. The ground was bare and we sat and talked. I asked the girls their favorite gift of Christmases past.

Emma remembered a wooden horse shed, built by her father. She kept a palomino there, with wheels on its feet. Skye remembered a doll's crib Steve made the same year. "I'd forgotten those," Steve said.

He remembers Christmas 12 years ago when Skye was born, on the 23rd. Every year he opened a bottle of dandelion wine brewed that summer. Emma, then, 3, had helped gather blossoms. There were only half a dozen bottles left.

"It's a delightful vintage that's increasingly special to me," Steve said. "An irreplaceable vintage."

By the time we got back it was dark. I warmed up briefly and packed to go. Emma, padding in her socks, said how nice it was to be home.

"That's why we go out and get cold," Steve laughed. "To come home."

That evening they planned to sculpt and bake a crèche of clay. It would be a quiet time.

"I feel incredibly fortunate and blessed," Steve said in parting. "Intensely happy."

I roared off through the night, the little headlight bouncing on the snow. It took an hour-and-a-half to reach my cabin in West Yellowstone. I called Steve to say I had made it.

I turned on the Christmas lights, put on Christmas music and wrapped presents. A few cards had arrived, and I read them by the fire.

What a wonderful time. Family. Friends. The warmth of coming home.

DECEMBER 27

- - -

Christmas is a gift in itself to the towns that circle Yellowstone National Park. It is the start of the winter season, a second chance at tourist dollars.

Enthralled by the beauty of Yellowstone in winter and the ring of cash registers, all will be peace and good cheer in these gateways to the park.

By season's end, though, the combination of cabin fever and Dickens' greed will set these towns to fighting among themselves — and with the park — over the richness of Yellowstone. And the combination will provide another example of how gateways, which owe their existence to the park, try to control it.

Starting this week, dogs no longer can sleep in West Yellowstone streets, as they did in November. The streets, now snow-covered, are busy with bubble-headed creatures astride motorized sleds — crotch rockets, some call them. They are parked at cafes, gas stations, and motels, and each morning I can hear their whines through the log walls of my cabin.

It will be that way until spring when tourists in RVs on wheels awaken and begin to head to Yellowstone. But RVs can't get into the park until the roads are plowed. And plowing roads ends the snowmobile season. That's where the conflict lies.

West Yellowstone wants the lucrative snowmobile season extended. The other gateways, Cooke City, Cody, and Jackson, want traffic, and traditional tourist dollars, to flow. One town's gain is another's loss.

Last March, deposits in West Yellowstone's bank during the peak snowmobile week were $1.1 million. Deposits the first week of April, when the park closed to snowmobiles and plowing began for automobiles, were $376,000.

By contrast, businesses in Cooke City, the northeast corner, make thousands of dollars each week the roads are open. Cooke City is a cold cul de sac in winter, cut off from the east by huge drifts across Beartooth Pass. Its 75 winter souls count the days until spring, when the park opens the road.

Last spring, when plowing was delayed, people in Cooke City and Red Lodge got out scoop shovels and snowblowers and began digging the road clear, making a symbolic dent in the snowpack.

Caught in the middle of this conflict, literally, is the park. This spring, under a compromise, the park will plow roads to the east, but leave snow on the road to West Yellowstone a little longer. So important is it to merchants in West Yellowstone that they have agreed to help pay overtime to the snowplow drivers.

The conflict in spring is a good example, I think, of the pulls on the park by its gateway communities. Sometimes the conflict reminds me of spoiled children fighting over an inheritance.

The gateway communities owe a large measure of their success — if not their existence — to the richness of this park. West Yellowstone, for example, was started as a train depot and entrance. Yet they act, sometimes, as if they owned it, and exert tremendous influence on park policies.

A case in point is Cody's success in keeping Fishing Bridge facilities open when the park wanted to give it back to grizzly bears. The fact that one of Wyoming's senators is from Cody, and sits on a committee controlling park budgets, didn't go unnoticed at park headquarters.

Cody has a world class museum but is 50 miles from the park. If tourists heading west don't stop — and one survey showed half of them don't — Cody never sees them again.

Fishing Bridge is the first stop in the park at the Cody entrance, and closing the campground and store, Cody fears, would give people another reasons to bypass their town.

All national parks draw people. And snagging tourists as they pass into or out of a park always has been a good way to make a living.

But Yellowstone is an environmental symbol to the nation, and it's sad to have neighbors who see it as a source of income, only.

DECEMBER 28

\- - -

It's difficult to get a room at Old Faithful now. The road along the Firehole is moguled and rough from so many snowmobiles. Cross-country skiers are everywhere. Yellowstone's winter season is in full swing, and I have run out of adjectives to describe it. It is something everyone should see.

I'm afraid they will.

When I first came to Yellowstone last May, I went for a walk with naturalist Jack de Golia. Snow was still on the ground, and he showed me how to see signs of spring.

An obvious sign, for him, was the arrival of people and an end to the "wilderness feeling." We talked about conflicts in Yellowstone, and he said something that haunts me now.

"If there's one thing that will save Yellowstone," he said, "it's winter."

Winter is a time of rest for Yellowstone. Bears and squirrels are hibernating. Birds have flown away. Plants are dormant.

Elk and buffalo have moved to winter range one-sixth the size of their summer pastures. They are living off their fat and what they can find on the ground. They are on a downhill slide, a naturalist told me, toward no fat and death.

To save their energy, buffalo and elk move to thermal areas, ridges and south slopes. They move slowly, for energy expended now could make the difference between life and death at winter's end.

Fourteen years ago, the first guests stayed overnight at Old Faithful. Today the 91 rooms are nearly always full, and rooms at the hotel in Mammoth are filling up after a year-end promotion of the winter season.

The question is, where does it go from here? When does too much winter use begin to damage the park?

It's a hot topic in cold Yellowstone. With 2 million visitors every summer there are many who look back on promotions in the 1960s as a mistake. Should national parks, charged with preserving nature, be in the business of promoting public use?

Yellowstone promotes its winter playground. It cuts ski trails. It employs full-time groomers to keep moguls down for snowmobilers. And it equips rangers with cold-weather gear, snowmobiles with radar, and kidney belts for the bumps.

Last winter, 100,000 people visited the park. Nearly half were on the 38,361 snowmobiles that roared through.

A study showed, however, that cross-country skiers displaced animals more than snowmobiles. The animals appeared to ignore snow machines that traveled predictably on the roads.

No one knows how much displacement would mean life or death to a buffalo come a hard winter. And what about solitude and quiet? Is there value in nature for that?

Park Superintendent Bob Barbee, an avid Nordic skier, says those questions should have been asked 20 years ago when snowmobiles were first allowed into the park. Now the snowmobilers have a vital interest in continuing the winter season, and they are a potent lobby.

Barbee also says a winter-use plan, now in its umpteenth revision, will not put a cap on winter use. There is a limit only, he said, on winterized overnight accommodations.

133

Yet TW Services, which runs the hotels and is a financial partner with the park, would like to winterize cabins to be built at Canyon, near the fragile Hayden Valley.

Yellowstone has survived for centuries, in part because of winter. The fact that we have learned to survive and play in the cold means the rules have changed.

I don't want to deprive anyone of seeing what I've seen this winter. Neither do I want it destroyed.

DECEMBER 31

- - -

I've spent the holidays putting on cholesterol and showing off the majesty of Yellowstone in winter.

On Christmas morning, after a huge breakfast, a friend and I watched Old Faithful erupt. From the fountain of hot water, a mushroom cloud of steam boiled and hung in the still blue air. It was as fine a gift as any I opened that day.

Today I'll take my daughter skiing at the edge of the Madison River, where the swans swim in mist, and snow drips from the edge like icing on a Bundt cake.

After dark we'll dine on soup made of leftover turkey. I'll settle down with a book by the fire, and before the New Year, will be asleep.

A couple of days ago, Rocky Barker, a reporter for the Idaho Falls newspaper, came to my cabin to interview me about Yellowstone. I guess if you stay in one place and pontificate long enough, somebody's bound to think you're an expert.

He never had seen Yellowstone in winter. I told him I'd rather be in the park showing him, than sitting in a cabin, talking about it. That's what I tried to do all summer and now — take people into the park.

Ultimately he asked *the* question, the one I set out to answer in May: What does Yellowstone mean to us?

I mumbled something about letting my letters from Yellowstone answer. He wasn't satisfied.

Well, I said, it means different things to different people. He didn't write that down, either.

People see and use the park in different ways, I continued. On foot in the backcountry, from the protection of an RV, at a picnic table, on a snowmobile. It's a very democratic park, in that sense.

I came to see Yellowstone as not just a wildlife preserve, but a place for people, too. A place to learn about the environment. A place where the political process mirrors our attitude toward the wild.

People, not biologists or environmentalists, will make the decisions about Yellowstone. And that's the way it should be.

He asked me if I was optimistic about the future of the park, and I said yes. I think people will preserve Yellowstone as a special place. Provided, as in any democratic process, that they get good information. And that, I hope, is where I helped.

This was an extraordinary opportunity for a journalist, to stay in one place for a third of a year. Steve Fuller, the winter keeper at the Grand Canyon, put it best. The longer one stays, the more one sees and understands.

In a few days, I'll return to my usual beat — roaming the Rockies. I'll come home for the Stock Show, then go to the Southwest for a while.

I'd like to meet a Texas Ranger, spend some time along the border, and talk to Southwestern artists. Along about spring, when the snow in the Rockies begins to melt, I plan to write about water.

As I move about from one motel room to another, I'll take with me the magic of Yellowstone, memories that lie like peaks and valleys in a mountain range.

I'll take with me, too, a new picture book I bought here. Something to satisfy the other side of the wandering me.

Its title is "American Log Homes."

AFTERWORD

A visitor making their first trip to Yellowstone National Park will find a landscape as wondrous as Jim Carrier described over a year-long visit to America's natural pilgrimage.

Its steaming, sulfurous thermal features, mountain peaks, wild rivers and grand canyon are as unique today as their were for members of the 1870 Washburn expedition and other visitors like, John Muir, Chief Joseph and President Barack Obama and his family. But Carrier's Yellowstone 1987 was on the precipice of a great transformation of geologic proportions.

Jim would join me the next summer as more than 700,000 acres of the national park and surrounding national forests burned in America's first megafire since the great fires of 1910. Those Yellowstone blazes captured the nation's attention and on September 7, 1988 caught up to Jim and me at Old Faithful.

He led us to the safety of the large parking lot in front of the Old Faithful Inn as the firestorm, which unleashed energy comparable to a nuclear explosion, raged through the area. We survived but it wouldn't be long before giant fires like those in Yellowstone in 1988 became routine across the West, forcing thousands to flee. The Yellowstone Fires of 1988 were the signal fires of climate change caused by the burning of fossil fuels since the dawn of the Industrial age. Since then megafires have burned nearly half of the Northern Rockies and through communities from Colorado Springs, San Diego to Santa Rosa.

Yellowstone is hotter, especially in the spring and at night. The time between the last freeze of the spring to the first of the fall has grown by nearly 30 days since Jim ranged through the park in 1987. The runoff comes earlier and the snow melts faster, changing the biological clock for everything from the hibernating grizzly bears to migrating bison and the returning song birds and pollinators. This extraordinary rapid warming trend will continue at least until the end of this century even if human civilization succeeds to shifting to an economy free of carbon and greenhouse gas production.

That means the forest that has regrown since 1988 will likely burn again and again until Ponderosa pines grow where lodgepole dominate today.

Then there is the volcanic action that created the geysers, hot pots and fumeroles that are the main attraction. Old Faithful's interval has grown from 72 minutes on average in 1987 to 90 to 92 minutes today. In 2011 scientists said the ground above the magma reservoir that heats the water rose 11 inches in seven years.

The reservoir itself is two and half times what geologists believed before increasing the still long odds for a supervolcano eruption.

Yellowstone visitation has grown annually to more than 4 million people since 2015 but an increasing number come from overseas. The park fee has risen to $30 a car and could double if the Interior secretary gets his way.

Wolves were returned to the park in 1995 reversing a century of long outdated idea that fewer predators would mean more elk and deer. Today the elk population is healthy and growing, biologists say.

More than 700 grizzly bears roam the greater Yellowstone ecosystem and like wolves, the population has been delisted as threatened under the Endangered Species Act. Seeing wild grizzlies in the park is a regular event that visitors can depend on if they stay for more than a couple of days.

The success stories of wolves and grizzlies shows what we can accomplish in conservation even in the midst of growing visitor numbers. But uncertainty remains over what carrying capacity is for this place that will change dramatically before the end of this century due to our worldwide impact.

Jim came to Yellowstone at the end of one chapter in the park's history and he showed why it remains a spiritual mecca as well as a scientific baseline and fun place to visit. He told the story of Steve Fuller, the last of the winterkeepers who lived in isolation for years at Canyon Village in the winter as he raised his family, photographed its beauty and became a part of his surroundings.

After 45 years Fuller remains at Canyon, staring into the abyss of Yellowstone's Grand Canyon still, watching hot springs form crystals that rise up in the sunrise light with the same sense of wonder he had when he arrived in 1973.

His joy, like John Muir's and Jim Carrier's, comes from the wildness we can still find and celebrate in this revered ground.

Rocky Barker © (2018)
*Rocky Barker has covered environmental issues
in and around Yellowstone for 43 years.*

REVIEW

Throughout the summer, fall, and winter of 1986 I eagerly
awaited each issue of *The Denver Post* that contained Jim Carrier's
latest "Letter from Yellowstone." At the time, the reading of these
marvelous narratives was somewhat bittersweet; I always thought it
was a shame that such wonderful writing about the most most
important national park in the world would ultimately be lost to
posterity. Now, thanks to publisher Roberts Rinehart, all seventy
letters have been saved and bound together in one lovely volume,
handsomely illustrated with fine watercolors by Robert Spannring.

In reading this fascinating account of one man's year in
Yellowstone National Park, one quickly runs out of superlatives.
Carrier writes with sensitivity, intelligence, and maturity about the
magnificent beauty of this Wyoming wilderness and its wildlife. He
also provides some of the best written accounts I have seen yet on
the many controversial problems currently besetting the park: the
fate of the endangered grizzly bear, the damage resulting from
excessive recreational use, the challenge of thermal drilling outside
the park, and the possibility of wolf restoration, to name just a few.

Carrier writes:

*There is a saying I hear often from people who love the parks
and forests: "Once it's gone, it's gone. They don't mean the whole
tapestry, I now realize. Their concern is with each thread, being
pulled one at a time. There will always be a Yellowstone. The
question is, how rich and beautiful — how valuable — will it be?"*

Many years ago, while an undergraduate at the University of
Colorado, I had the chance to work for a summer as a horse wrangler
at a dude ranch just outside Yellowstone National Park. I will never
forget our long pack trips through the Absaroka Wilderness, looking
always toward the giant snow-capped peaks of the park just to the
west. Jim Carrier was lucky enough to be able to spend almost an

entire year living in a place that is as close to heaven as any I've seen.

Letters from Yellowstone has already become something of a minor classic of western nature writing and is a fitting tribute to our most beloved, and in many ways our most endangered, national park. So long as the park has interpreters and defenders as eloquent and committed as Jim Carrier, there is hope that our children and their children will also be able to know the sights we hold so dear: a herd of wild bison thundering over the expansive grasslands of Hayden Valley, a giant silvertip bear lumbering off into the lodgepoles with her two cubs bouncing behind, a pair of pure white trumpeter swans taking flight over a lonely lake in the deep timber. These scenes are as much a part of our freedom as any word in the Constitution, and need to be defended with the same resoluteness. A hearty thanks from this reviewer to Jim Carrier for writing the book, to *The Denver Post* for supporting his work, and to Roberts Rinehart for publishing *Letters from Yellowstone.*

John Murray
Bloomsbury Review July 7, 1988
John Murray has published numerous nature books, including the
Sierra Club's handbook, "Writing About Nature: A creative guide."

EPILOGUE

In the mind of a child,

what remains after a trip through Yellowstone?

I like to tell people that my dad had one of the coolest jobs in journalism: he got to drive around the Rockies and write stories. He lived in Yellowstone, on a ranch, with a Native American family; he climbed the Tetons and rafted the Grand Canyon. He met interesting people and told their stories.

I was fortunate enough to go along on some of those adventures. I've seen more of the West than most, usually from the passenger seat of Dad's Jeep. I remember how happy he was when I turned 16, because I could drive while he reviewed notes and typed his stories. My love of road trips is due entirely to those hours with him – even though I'm sure I complained about them at the time.

To an eleven-year-old with a love of the outdoors, a summer in Yellowstone is pure magic. The park was the world's best back yard and playground, and it was all mine. I was young enough to not have many responsibilities, yet old enough to appreciate what was available to me. I was, in a word, blessed.

So what does stay in the mind after a childhood summer in Yellowstone? Bright images, like shining pearls, to be treasured and brought out occasionally to admire.

I remember our nighttime hike around the geysers, hearing the strangest of noises – like a dragon growling, or perhaps belching – coming from the very heart of the planet. Dad's version of the story does not include his mock threat to toss me in to see who lived down there.

I remember our hike into bear country with Bill Jordan and Jerry Lewis, when Bill fell and couldn't use his leg. Dad tells of his hike back out in the middle of the night to get help, but what he wasn't there to see was me sitting by a dying fire while Jerry went to scrounge up more firewood. I was convinced that Bill's groans of pain were like duck calls for bears. I kept expecting a large pair of eyes to appear in the underbrush. I would have been the appetizer, or maybe dessert.

I remember spending the day with Rick Hutchinson, learning about geysers and the geology of Yellowstone. For the rest of the summer – and the next few years – I was determined I would be a geologist. I still think it would be a cool career, and I'm still fascinated by rocks. Somewhere I have a shadow box with specimens from that time.

I remember thinking how cool it was that I got to meet people like Rick, and see the "back story" of Yellowstone – things that the everyday visitor didn't have access to. I developed a bit of a swagger around other kids; I was (I'm sure) an insufferable know-it-all.

I remember the family that came and stayed in a nearby campground; there were three kids who had never been to Yellowstone before. We would ride our bikes around town; one afternoon the whole family and I piled into the van to drive around the park. I neglected to tell Dad where I was going; upon my return hours later he wanted to know if seeing the park with them was better than when I was with him. I think I was getting on his nerves; after sitting through numerous interviews I confess I was impatient and was likely acting my age (pre-teen boredom is a dangerous thing).

I remember the traffic – daytrippers who had given themselves four or six hours to see the park before hurrying on to their next destination. They missed so much while they clogged up the roads. To this day I scowl and mutter under my breath whenever I see an RV, though I will now join the crowd on the road's shoulder, hoping for a glimpse of a moose.

I remember the owner of the little cabin community we lived in in West Yellowstone. A grandpa-like figure who tolerated my many questions, he "hired" me to mow the grass around the cabins every week (my first job). He would pay me with silly tin commemorative coins that were good at a few shops in town. I'd treat Dad to an ice cream (on a waffle cone!); he thought my mix of Mexican vanilla and Whoppers was disgusting.

I remember our ski-doo ride into the park at Christmas; it was COLD. And snowing. I still have a picture of Old Faithful, right on time, steam and snowflakes in the air.

I remember – though I didn't recognize it then – how special it was to have this time with my dad. At the time, that's who he was – Dad – but as I grew older I began to recognize him as an individual with many talents and accomplishments, who loves to travel and learn and ask questions. I've had people tell me that I have a true curiosity about others – where they're from, what they care about; I thank them for the compliment and tell them that I come by it honestly.

I remember the smell of pine trees and wildflowers, the glow of sunsets and the chirp of chickadees in the early mornings. I remember campfires and marshmallows; vegetable soup cooked on the wood stove and cornbread out of a skillet. I remember the creeks and Yellowstone River, where the dragonflies hovered and waterbugs skittered across; I wished I could dance across the water like them. I remember how breathtaking the park is during a thunderstorm – the word majestic is not a cliché.

And I remember the taste of our dinner of trout and bread – a meal I still enjoy, and which never fails to make me think of my summer in Yellowstone with Dad.

Amy L. Carrier, PhD

Amy Carrier is Senior Director, Advancement Information Management, Oregon State University Foundation

Made in the USA
Middletown, DE
19 January 2019